SPIRITUAL PLACES

SPIRITUAL PLACES

THE WORLD'S MOST SACRED SITES

ANTONY MASON

Quercus

CONTENTS

Introduction 6

Stonehenge, UK 8
Lindisfarne, UK 12
Carnac, France 16
Cathar ruins, France 20
Chartres Cathedral, France 24
Omaha Beach, France 28
Lascaux, France 32
Lourdes, France 34
Vatican City, Italy 38
Borgund stave church, Norway 42
Santiago de Compostela, Spain 44
La Mezquita de Córdoba, Spain 48
Fátima, Portugal 52
Mount Athos, Greece 56
Parthenon, Greece 60
Sergiyev Posad, Russia 64
Church of the Saviour on the Spilled Blood,
    Russia 68
Temple of Heaven, China 72
Wudang Mountains, China 74
Potala Palace, Tibet, China 78
Mount Fuji, Japan 82
Kinkaku-ji, Japan 86
Angkor Wat, Cambodia 90
Mahabodhi Temple, India 94
Varanasi, India 96
The Golden Temple of Amritsar, India 100
Taj Mahal, India 104
Uluru, Australia 108
Golden Rock, Burma 110
Mount Agung, Bali 112
Borobudur, Indonesia 116
Mecca, Saudi Arabia 120
Petra, Jordan 124
Sea of Galilee, Israel 128
Dome of the Rock, Israel 130
Blue Mosque, Turkey 134
Mount Ararat, Turkey 138
Gorëme, Cappadocia, Turkey 142
Samarkand, Uzbekistan 146
Karnak, Egypt 148
Mount Sinai, Egypt 152
Lalibela, Ethiopia 156
Great Mosque of Djenné, Mali 160
Chichén Itzá, Mexico 164
Palenque, Mexico 168
Machu Picchu, Peru 172
Lake Titicaca, Peru/Bolivia 176
Superstition Mountain, USA 180
Crater Lake, USA 182
Chaco Canyon, USA 186

Index 190
Acknowledgements 192

12 Lindisfarne

8 Stonehenge

28 Omaha Beach

16 Carnac

52 Fátima

48 La Mezquita de Córdoba

182 Crater Lake

186 Chaco Canyon

180 Superstition Mountain

164 Chichén Itzá

168 Palenque

160 Great Mosque of Djenné

172 Machu Picchu

176 Lake Titicaca

42 Borgund stave church

68 Church of the Saviour on the Spilled Blood

64 Sergiyev Posad

24 Chartres Cathedral

32 Lascaux

134 Blue Mosque

20 Cathar ruins

142 Gorëme

146 Samarkand

72 Temple of Heaven

82 Mount Fuji

38 Vatican City

138 Mount Ararat

100 The Golden Temple of Amritsar

56 Mount Athos

128 Sea of Galilee

78 Potala Palace

86 Kinkaku-ji

60 Parthenon

124 Petra

74 Wudang Mountains

94 Mahabodhi Temple

34 Lourdes

104 Taj Mahal

44 Santiago de Compostela

96 Varanasi

110 Golden Rock

120 Mecca

130 Dome of the Rock

156 Lalibela

90 Angkor Wat

152 Mount Sinai

112 Mount Agung

148 Karnak

116 Borobudur

108 Uluru

INTRODUCTION

Spiritual places clearly have a quality that sets them apart. But trying to define that special quality is self-defeating. Spiritual places, and our experiences of them, ultimately belong in a domain beyond words. The best of them are sublime, and all the others are on that spectrum: they are portals, if not to another world, then at least to another part of our brains. They take us out of our mundane, routine worlds of work, the internet, advertising, banking, supermarkets, and place us in a different sphere – more vital, more important, closer to the eternal. They provide a fresh, therapeutic perspective on our daily lives and make them bearable.

Spiritual places are usually assigned to the realm of religion but conventional religion may struggle to lay claim to them: they may not be easily pigeonholed. Only human beings have created religions, or, as the faithful might say, have been vouchsafed religions by their god or gods. Religions have the answers to the big questions and mysteries of life – how to bring and maintain good fortune, what happens after death, why we are here. That is, you could argue, their origin and their main function. And that is why, so often, they are attached to spiritual places.

But do spiritual places have a quality independent of religion – which pre-dates religion? What first distinguishes a spiritual place and gives it a special sanctity? It could perhaps simply have been exceptional natural beauty – a mountain, a lake or a stand of trees with the power to entrance. Perhaps it had a vital use, such as a spring, of such life-and-death importance that it inspired devotion. Maybe some memorable event occurred at this place, such as a death or burial, or some kind of unexplained psychic experience – a vision or a dream. Or perhaps it was associated with a special power, identifying it as lucky, or capable of healing. Any such tag could enter the collective memory, investing a place with special significance, inviting reverence. And if a place had such special significance, maybe this was where human beings could influence their own destiny by showing respect to – and performing rituals in honour of – the source of its power, to the spirits or gods or supernatural forces that were presumed to be attached to it.

Several of the most powerful spiritual places are raw, unadorned natural phenomena – essentially awe-inspiring in their own right. Places like Uluru, Mount Fuji and Crater Lake have probably been held sacred since human beings first set eyes on them and before they could evolve ways to make sense of their emotional response to them through myth and religion. The sites themselves – because of their startlingly unusual qualities – probably provoked the suggestion that they could not have been made simply by the random forces of nature: some greater power was at work here.

The oldest uniquely prehistoric spiritual place in this book is the Lascaux Caves in France, painted some 17,000 years ago by people who depended for their survival on hunting. Their focus in their art on animals that would provide them with food suggests that they might have hoped that the images had some positive or magical influence on the outcome of their hunting. When our ancestors turned from hunting to agriculture after about 7000 BC, the passing of the seasons took on greater significance: the success of their crops depended upon the relationship of the earth to the heavens, which was mapped by the changing pattern of the stars. Ancient megalithic monuments such as Stonehenge and Carnac suggest that colossal collective effort was marshalled to create lines, rings and structures of stone that could track and mark the solstices – particularly the winter solstice that signalled the turn of the year towards light and warmth.

By definition, prehistoric monuments left no written records. The motivation that lay behind the effort to transport huge stones across vast distances can only be a matter of speculation. Our interpretation comes largely from later monuments born of equally colossal collective effort, but here the motivation was much clearer. The temple of Karnak in Ancient Egypt, the Buddhist temple of Borobudur, and the cathedral of Chartres, all – in their different ways – were structures designed as complex expressions of highly developed religions. If they were not actually inhabited by gods, they were built to channel communications with the gods. They were also ambitious acts of bravado, with murderously high human costs. Until relatively recently, just about all such mega-structures had a religious purpose, and thus we assume that Stonehenge and Carnac did so too. On the basis of human experience since written history began, we have no convincing counter-argument.

Many of the world's most sacred places have a centuries-old history. The Masjid al-Haram in Mecca was built around the Ka'aba, whose history is said to date back to Abraham, the patriarch who – if a historical character – is thought to have lived some time between 2000 and 1650 BC. Córdoba's cathedral is a former mosque whose columns were salvaged from Roman and Visigothic ruins. Chartres Cathedral was built on the site of a well sacred to the Druids. But age is by no means an essential ingredient. New spiritual places can arise quite suddenly to take on a profound significance. Lourdes (from 1858) and Fatíma (from 1917), both places formerly unknown to the world at large, developed rapidly as the focus of international pilgrimage out of visionary experiences that occurred unexpectedly and lasted a mere matter of months.

Pilgrimage lends additional weight to any spiritual place, as if the effort of individuals to make this devotional journey, multiplied many millions of times across the centuries, reinforces its value and significance. Several of the world's greatest pilgrimage sites are places where critical historical religious events occurred, such as Bodh Gaya, where the Buddha achieved enlightenment; the Sea of Galilee, where Jesus performed much of his ministry, and many of his most famous miracles; Mecca, the birthplace of the Prophet Muhammad, and where he received the first divine revelations of the Koran; and the Golden Temple of

Amritsar, which became the headquarters of Sikhism, and is where the holy book, the Sri Guru Granth Sahib, resides. Other places of pilgrimage were believed to be the site of some great, supernatural event recorded in scriptures or legend. At Varanasi, a city on the river that is the embodiment of the goddess Ganga, the great god Shiva arose in a fiery pillar of light to soar to the heavens; at Lake Titicaca, Viracocha, the supreme god of the Incas, emerged in the darkness to create the universe; Mount Sinai is where Moses encountered God at the burning bush, and later received the Ten Commandments; and the Dome of the Rock in Jerusalem marks the spot where Muhammad ascended to heaven on his Night Journey from Mecca.

Sacred relics or statues also attract pilgrims, promising blessings or healing or the forgiveness of past sins, or simply a sense of wellbeing. Such was the lure of Lindisfarne, and remains to this day the magnetic force of Santiago de Compostela and the Potala Palace. Often, however, it is the devotional effort of making the journey that is the greatest reward. The lure of pilgrimage is matched too by the commercial benefits that it has always offered to the place of pilgrimage, as well as to the stations all along the route: spiritual places are often cravenly exploited for their materialistic rewards.

Many of the most elaborate sacred structures are not simply shrines or places of worship, but physical symbols of the entire cosmology of a religion. This was the case of Karnak in Egypt, and Angkor Wat in Cambodia, and the Temple of Heaven in Beijing. By representing in miniature, and in an idealized form, the relationship and bond between heaven and earth, they invited the gods to channel their energies through them. Their careful construction reflects a profound belief in the essential order of the universe – which it was the god-king's duty to maintain by performing the correct rituals at the correct times. Calamity was not random, but the result of a failure to propitiate the gods satisfactorily. It was a knife-edge responsibility.

These are complex constructions, both of the physical world and of the mind. There are other spiritual places that instil a sense of awe and wonder for their astonishing beauty alone – beauty that transcends religion, or perhaps elevates religion to a new realm and carries us with it. The Parthenon, the Taj Mahal, Kinkaku-ji (the Golden Pavilion) all have this power. And words are not enough.

Antony Mason

Latitude 51°10'N **Longitude** 1°49'W	
Location Wiltshire, central southern England	
Faith Pagan	
Age 3,500–5,000 years	
Approximate area 0.8 hectares (2 acres)	
Access Ticketed entry normally restricted to a path on the western side	

STONEHENGE

Rising from a great, angled slab of grass-carpeted chalkland, surrounded by open farmland and distant clusters of wood, beneath a vast sky, there is something deeply elemental about Stonehenge. Crudely hewn, ancient, enigmatic, it seems to channel the weather into the landscape like a lightning rod. Nearly a million people visit Stonehenge – one of Britain's top historic attractions – every year. Many more glimpse it from car windows as they chase along the busy A303 that passes just to its south. It never fails to deliver a fresh shock of wonder.

There is nothing else quite like Stonehenge. It is the most complex and ambitious prehistoric megalithic structure in northern Europe. Some of its larger sarsen (sandstone) megaliths are 6 metres (20 ft) long and weigh 50 tonnes. Erected here at the end of the Stone Age, in about 2600 BC, they were probably dragged from the Marlborough Downs 40 kilometres (25 miles) away. This feat would, by some estimates, have required teams of some 600 workers for each stone. Earlier, in around 3000 BC, over 60 smaller 'bluestones' (the colour they go when wet) were, it seems, brought from the Preseli Hills in Wales, a journey that would have required dragging them on sleds overland and on rafts along rivers, over a distance of some 400 kilometres (250 miles).

Why? What was the purpose of this colossal endeavour? Nobody knows, but for centuries every generation has devised its own theory. In medieval times, legend explained Stonehenge as the magical creation of the wizard Merlin. In the 19th century, it was the temple of the Druids – but Druids arrived in Britain only in about 300 BC, when Stonehenge was already more than 2,000 years old.

The low sun is caught in the narrow gap between a pair of standing sarsen stones. Such moments suggest that Stonehenge may have functioned as an astronomical clock to track the advancing seasons.

TRAVELLER'S TIPS

Best time to go: Open every day except 24–25 December. Any time of year is good; bitter winter days are as atmospheric as sunlit summer ones.

Look out for: A free festival to celebrate the Summer Solstice (21 June) attracts huge 'New Age' crowds. The event is regulated by English Heritage and the police.

Dos and don'ts: Do not expect to have close access to the stones during a normal daytime visit. But you can enter the stone circle out of hours by booking through English Heritage.

There are no records beyond what can be discerned from the site itself. The stones clearly appear to have an alignment to astronomical phenomena, most notably to the positions of sunrise or sunset at the solstices. As Britain, when Stonehenge was created, depended increasingly on agriculture for survival, the progress of the seasons was of critical importance. Temple, observatory, giant calendar, ceremonial venue, cemetery for the élite – Stonehenge could have served any of these functions, or all of them together.

A recent theory has evolved from archaeological work at a nearby site called Durrington Walls, a large Neolithic (New Stone Age) village that has yielded a huge number of beef and pork bones. Analysis of the remains suggests that the village was seasonally occupied, over a short period of 45 years or so in about 2500 BC, by around 4,000 people, some of whom may have come from as far away as the Scottish islands. So was this the workforce, gathering from all over the land to toil and feast and celebrate the winter solstice?

But why here? The earliest manifestation of Stonehenge – well before the arrival of the rings of lintelled standing stones we see today – was the circular bank and ditch that still girdles the site, dating from about 3000 BC. Positioned all around the rim were 56 pits containing cremated human remains, formerly marked by standing bluestones that were later moved. Whoever created such an elaborate burial site had clearly made a choice to locate it here. A broad, straight processional avenue, flanked by banks, leads up to the circle: it points to the position of sunset at the midwinter solstice. This avenue may in fact have been a natural phenomenon, a fluke creation of the glaciers of the Ice Age. Perhaps it was this that marked the site as special to the very first founders of Stonehenge.

In around 2500 BC, work on Stonehenge ceased. But the area still clearly retained special significance. The surrounding landscape became dotted with round barrows – mounds marking the elaborate graves of the so-called Beaker People (after their ceramic grave goods), indicative of a cultural shift. This part of England is crowded with similar prehistoric monuments: burial sites, the extensive megalithic complex of the Avebury Rings, the monumental artificial mound of Silbury Hill. Stonehenge – perhaps the focus of national power and religious observance – remains the most impressive of them all.

There is a strong spirit of place here, resonating from the brutal antiquity of the stones, from the breezes that rustle the grasses and bend the crops in the fields, from the scudding clouds overhead. Although – or because – its meaning eludes us, Stonehenge still commands respect and awe today, as it has done for more than 5,000 years.

Only about 40 per cent of Stonehenge remains standing, but the original structure can be deduced from two concentric rings of stones. The word 'henge' may refer to the cross-pieces known as 'hanging stones' because of their resemblance to gallows.

LINDISFARNE

Latitude 55°40'N **Longitude** 1°47'W

Location Northumberland, northeast England

Faith Christian

Built From 7th century AD

Approximate area 4 square kilometres (1.6 sq miles)

Access Tides restrict access to the island; ticketed entry to the priory and castle

On bright sunny days, the low-lying island of Lindisfarne sits like a soft brushstroke of watercolour dividing the sparkling sea from a long arc of the blue sky tufted with cloud. Wild flowers nod among the dry, rustling marram grass: sea campion, red valerian, thrift, tiny orchids. A tarmacked causeway crosses the mudflats tying the island to the Northumbrian mainland just 1.5 kilometres (1 mile) away, but twice a day the tide rises and submerges it for five hours, cutting off traffic, and the intrusion of the outside world. Lindisfarne exudes a deep peace, held in the timeless interaction between landscape and the forces of nature.

This must have been part of the attraction for early Christian monks, who first settled here in AD 635. They were led by St Aidan, who arrived from Ireland via the monastery at Iona, in western Scotland. But St Aidan and his 12 brethren had not come to retreat into meditative isolation. They had been invited to Lindisfarne by the king of Northumbria, St Oswald, to spread Christianity among his heathen subjects. Britain had been nominally Christian at the end of the Roman era, but after the Romans left in the fifth century, paganism re-emerged. Of all northern Europe, only in Ireland, and later in isolated outposts such as Iona, did the light of Christianity still burn.

Far from being isolated, Lindisfarne was, in fact, on the main and most reliable thoroughfare of the day: the sea. From here St Aidan and his missionaries travelled far and wide, and deep inland into the north of England. After St Aidan died at Lindisfarne in AD 651, his successors continued his work with increased vigour. Notable among them was St Cuthbert

TRAVELLER'S **TIPS**

Best time to go: Late spring for its wild flowers and scintillating light (when sunny). The castle is closed November to mid-March and on Mondays.

Look out for: The Lindisfarne Centre has an interactive replica of the illuminated Lindisfarne Gospels. The focus for pilgrims today is the 12th-century Anglican Church of St Mary the Virgin.

Dos and don'ts: Consult the tide tables posted at each end. Don't begin crossing on the Pilgrim's Way (on foot) if the tide is rising.

The 16th-century castle rises on its rugged knoll of rock on the southeastern corner of the island. In the early 20th century its ruins were reconstructed to make a country house, to designs by Sir Edwin Lutyens.

The 11th-century priory flourished for 500 years until, in 1537, it was destroyed in the Dissolution of the Monasteries that followed Henry VIII's secession from the Catholic Church of Rome. These are the evocative ruins that we see today.

(c.634–87), who was said to have seen a vision, while tending his sheep, of St Aidan rising to heaven. After wide-ranging missionary work, he became Bishop of Lindisfarne in 684, but died three years later. His alleged ability to perform miracles during his lifetime seems to have been transferred to his tomb, which became the focus of pilgrimage, and Lindisfarne earned its other name: Holy Island. It was now becoming one of the main monastic centres in England. The exquisite illuminated manuscript called the Lindisfarne Gospels (now in the British Museum) was made here in about 700.

As a pacifist community exposed to the sea, Lindisfarne caught the eye of marauders. The Vikings attacked and sacked Lindisfarne in 793, an event that sent shockwaves throughout Britain and cemented that date as the start of the Viking era. The monks soldiered on through repeated attacks, but abandoned the island in 875; St Cuthbert's relics were transferred to Durham Cathedral for safekeeping. Later, after the conquest of Britain by the Normans (descendants of the Vikings) in the 11th century, a new monastery known as Lindisfarne Priory was built.

This island on the northern cusp of England has an enduring spirit of place that still attracts pilgrims. Many of them come on foot across the sands at low tide, along the 5-kilometre (3-mile) Pilgrim's Way, marked by tall poles. Large, box-like refuges, perched on stilts, offer a lifeline if any walkers are caught out by rising tides – a reminder of the untamed forces of nature that are part of the essence of this Holy Island.

An old tradition on Lindisfarne, and the UK's east coast generally, was to use redundant boats as sheds. Rather than being simply left to rot in the water, old keelboats that had become unsafe for seafaring were simply brought ashore, upturned and truncated, fitted with endwalls and doors, and the hulls covered or treated to make them weatherproof. The juncture between land and sea on Lindisfarne is seamless.

CARNAC

Beyond where knowledge runs out lie mystery and wonder. Religion often steps in with an explanation. But where there is no religion to offer that service, we are left just with that mystery and wonder – and a sense of spirituality without a religion to frame it.

That is certainly the case at Carnac. Between about 4500 and 2000 BC – probably mainly around 3300 BC – thousands of huge stones, or megaliths, were dragged to the site and erected in straight or gently curving lines. They march across heather-strewn moorland, across fields and through woodland, past the farms and churches of later generations, heading towards the sea. The main sequence, or set of alignments, stretches over a distance of 4 kilometres (2.5 miles) and contains some 3,000 stones – or menhirs as they are known (Breton *men*, stone, and *hir*, long) – often ten or more ranks deep. It consists of four groups: the largest to the west called Ménec and Kermario; and the smaller Kerlescan and Petit-Ménec farther to the northeast. Between them are various enclosure-like rings or squares of stones called cromlechs.

The Kermario Dolmen is a classic megalithic grave, set among the standing stone alignment of the same name. Originally this would have been covered (we assume) by a large mound of earth, but this has been washed away over time, laying bare a colossal table-like structure with capstones set on vertical pillars – a form that gave rise to the name dolmen (from the Breton *dol*, meaning 'table' and *men*, 'stone').

There is an elemental quality to the rough-hewn stones, standing with timeless solidity as the seasons rotate around them. Autumn brings russet colours to the surrounding landscape.

Their arrangement signifies some clear intention. But what? It has been puzzling people for centuries, and the font of all kinds of myths and legends. One says that Saint Cornély, the patron saint of cattle, who became Pope Cornelius in Rome (AD 251–253), was being chased by pagan Roman legions. Reaching the sea and with nowhere to go, he turned the soldiers into stone. The alignments certainly have a kind of military orderliness to them.

Colossal effort has been invested in these stones. In the alignments they vary in size up to about 4 metres (13 ft) high. Some of the isolated standing stones in the area are much larger still, such as the Géant du Manio, rising to 6.5 metres (21 ft). Roughly hewn from granite, and with the largest

weighing up to 280 tonnes, they would probably have been pulled into position on log rollers, then levered into a hole to make them point skywards. It would have required the kind of communal effort that was later marshalled to build the cathedrals of France. But at Carnac this effort was probably spread over many generations who shared the same vision, perhaps over a period of 1,000 years.

This was the Neolithic era, when Stone Age people had adopted farming – as opposed to hunting – as their main means of sustenance. The progression of the seasons, marked by the passage of solstices and equinoxes, was essential to survival. Could the Carnac alignments have been some kind of astronomical calendar? They seem to have lunar alignments,

often associated with cults of fertility. They may, on the other hand, have been memorials to the dead, to ancestors, or simply monuments to the gods. We will probably never know.

Many of the stones of Carnac have been decorated with engraved signs or symbols: swirls, sun-rays, axe-shapes, chevrons, snake-like forms. But this kind of finish was given in particular to stones within the tombs – and no more so than at 'Cairn' on the island of Gavrinis, to the east of Carnac, where polished stones are covered in large, fingerprint-like swirls and other images.

Such delicate marks, however, serve only to underline the bold, raw quality of the stones of Carnac: rough, natural

shapes that have clearly been selected and positioned with huge effort to mark a landscape. The big alignments make a deep impression because of the sheer numbers. But lonely sets of mossy stones encountered along woodland paths, as in the forest of Petit-Ménec, have a mystery of another kind, speaking of our ancestors' close, vital and elemental bond with nature. We may not know their religion, but we can share their spirituality.

Shapes, sizes and spacing of the stones vary considerably, sometimes wide and gappy, sometimes tightly packed, as if to form a wall-like barrier. The scale of the whole enterprise tends to dwarf the immense effort required to raise even the smaller stones.

TRAVELLER'S TIPS

Best time to go: Any time of year, but note that Carnac is also a summer beach resort and the stones are a huge tourist attraction. In October–March you can have free access to the alignments.

Look out for: The Musée de Préhistoire in Carnac has a huge collection of 6,600 archaeological artefacts (pottery, jewellery, weapons, tools) recovered from the prehistoric sites, plus maps and models.

Dos and don'ts: Wear good walking shoes. Many of the best moments occur at remote sites, away from the crowds, accessed by rural and woodland paths. Take a torch to see inside the dolmens.

Four castles make up the ensemble called the Châteaux de Lastours, which belonged to the Lords of Cabaret, who offered protection to the Cathars. The castles were subject to repeated attack for 20 years until they finally fell in 1229.

Latitude 43°12'N Longitude 2°21'E

Location Around the department of Aude, southwest France

Faith Christian

Built 11th–13th century

Approximate area 15,000 square kilometres (6,000 sq miles)

Access Some ticketed, open only Easter to September; others freely open at all times

CATHAR RUINS

On remote, isolated hilltops across southwest France stand the gaunt ruins of some 30 'Cathar castles'. An air of tragedy hangs over them: they were the last refuges of a peaceable medieval Christian sect who dared to think differently, but who were brutally persecuted and crushed by the Catholic Church and the forces that supported it.

Catharism arose in part as a reaction against the stranglehold that the Catholic Church had gained over religious beliefs and practices across Europe; the Church was also perceived as corrupt, and disconnected from the teachings of Christ and the Gospels. The word Cathar comes from the Greek *katharoi*, meaning 'the pure'. At heart, the Cathars had a belief system that differed fundamentally from Catholicism. Life, as they saw it, was the battleground of two forces: God, who was an invisible, eternal force for good, versus Evil, which was embodied in the material world of day-to-day reality. Human beings were material things, and therefore essentially evil, but could escape to God by transcending the material world, which meant renouncing all physical appetites and pleasures. The few who strictly followed that course took vows at an initiation and became known as 'perfects'. They were celibate and, as the taking of life was forbidden, ate no meat. The rest of the people could lead relatively free and liberal lives, but when close to death they could receive a sacrament called the Consolamentum, which would guarantee them salvation if they did not subsequently sin. It was a religion of the people, where individuals were empowered to take control of their own spiritual destiny.

By the 12th century Catharism had taken a firm hold in the Languedoc region of southwest France, which was then still an autonomous borderland between the kingdom of France and Aragon in Spain. Here the Cathars were supported by the

TRAVELLER'S TIPS

Best time to go: Any time of year, but spring (April–May) and autumn (September) are most pleasant. Southwest France can be intensely hot in July–August.

Look out for: Cathare cheese, made from goat's milk in the Languedoc region, with a Cathar cross stencilled on the surface in charcoal – a measure of the affection in which the Cathars are still held.

Dos and don'ts: Don't imagine that the castles have uniquely Cathar histories; they have served other military purposes throughout the centuries and may bear the scars of quite different events and struggles.

ruling nobles, such as Count Raymond VI of Toulouse. Catharism was condemned as heretical by the Catholic Church at the Council of Toulouse in 1119. Pope Innocent III attempted to persuade the Cathars back into the fold, but when, in 1209, his Papal Legate was assassinated in Toulouse, he chose to use force. The French king of the day, Philip II Augustus, saw this as an opportunity to make a grab for Languedoc. The result was a series of brutal sieges, massacres and mass executions. In 1209 some 20,000 people were put to the sword at Béziers, men, women and children. The tale is told that soldiers at Béziers were concerned that they were killing Catholics as well as Cathars, to which the Papal Legate, the Abbot of Citeaux, responded chillingly, 'Kill them all. God will know his own.'

The Crusade officially came to an end in 1229, with the Treaty of Paris. France, now under King Louis IX, had gained control over Languedoc. But the persecution of Cathars continued. Surviving communities took refuge in the castles of the lords who protected them, but they were gradually picked off and destroyed. The Cathars today are remembered with wistful nostalgia in southwest France, and their ruins now stand as monuments to resistance against the establishment, and the brutal force of centralized authority.

Although labelled 'Cathar', the castles had a history either side of the Cathar episode, and were built and maintained like any other medieval fortresses for strategic military purposes. The Château of Quéribus, for instance, served as a border post between France and Aragon. Its spiral staircases descended anticlockwise to give the advantage of space to defenders with swords in their right hands against attackers coming up.

Part of the romance of the Cathar castles is the remote beauty of their setting. The château of Quéribus – one of their last refuges, which fell in 1255 – stands on a high peak, with dramatic views for miles around.

CHARTRES CATHEDRAL

The Victorians were enthralled by magic lanterns: vivid pictures telling stories projected through painted glass onto a wall in a darkened room. Six centuries earlier the people of the French town of Chartres stepped into a vast magic lantern built of stone when they entered their cathedral. Sunlight penetrating from the outside projected rainbow shafts of light through walls filled with stained glass, scattering shards of colour across the floor and up the towering columns. There was no other experience quite like it: it was a vision of heaven.

And it still is. The Cathédrale Notre-Dame (Cathedral of Our Lady) is one of the world's best-preserved Gothic cathedrals, appearing more or less today as it did when it was consecrated to the Virgin Mary before King Louis IX in 1260. Most of its 172 windows still contain their original glass. Careful restoration has returned the walls and vaults to their original pale yellow and white colours, removing centuries of grime and candlewax soot.

When work began on the cathedral in 1194 it was at the cutting edge of architectural ambition. The plan was to build the highest cathedral ever, to replace the previous one, which had been destroyed by fire earlier that year. Some five cathedrals had stood here since the first one built during the early days of Roman Christianity, each successively destroyed through fire or violence. There is speculation, based on a reference by Julius Caesar, that the site may also have been

Latitude 48°26'N Longitude 1°29'E		
Location Central northern France		
Faith Christian (Roman Catholic)		
Built 12th and 13th centuries		
Approximate area 10,875 square metres (117,061 sq feet)		
Access Open daily, free (tickets for crypt)		

The elaborate encrustations of the cathedral's exterior stonework obscure the simple cruciform shape of the ground-plan, which can be seen only from the heavens.

The doors of the three bays of the Royal Portal at the western end of the cathedral are crowned with sculpture. The central bay shows Christ surrounded by the four Apocalyptic animals representing the four evangelists, Matthew, Mark, Luke and John.

held sacred by Druids in the pre-Christian era. Legend says that the bodies of early Christian martyrs were cast into a well here – which made it the focus of pilgrimage. The well can still be seen in the huge crypt, a vestige of the 12th-century predecessor of the current cathedral.

Chartres' appeal to pilgrims was enhanced further in AD 876 when King Charles the Bald (grandson of Charlemagne) donated the *Sancta Camisia*, the blouse said to have been worn by the Virgin Mary at the birth of Christ. As with many other cities across Europe, the economy of Chartres was closely bound to its fame as a pilgrimage site, which became a driving force in successive rebuildings of the cathedral. The rebuilding in 1145 had galvanized the people of Chartres into offering their services for free in a phenomenon called the 'Cult of the Carts': by pulling carts to ship stone to the worksite, they hoped to earn credit in heaven and be absolved of their sins.

Much the same happened in 1194–1250, when the current cathedral was being constructed.

But now it was different. No cathedral had ever been built like this before, so high and with so much of the walls filled with glass. The relatively recent innovation of the pointed Gothic arch provided a more vertical thrust, permitting more slender load-bearing columns, but the walls still had to take the weight of the roof. That was achieved by using cross-ribbed vaulting to make the ceiling lighter, and then by building flying buttresses outside to take the load – leaving the huge interior unprecedentedly spacious.

This provided the stage for the stained-glass makers: windows covering 2,600 square metres (28,000 sq ft). Their task was to turn Christianity into a visual experience, so the stories of the Bible could be recalled by – and recounted to – a mainly illiterate congregation. Noah's flood, the Nativity, the lives of the prophets and the saints, the Last Judgement and the coats of arms of aristocratic donors and the trades of the sponsoring guilds – all were vividly captured in glass, which included a newly invented, scintillating blue that has since been known as 'Chartres blue'.

In other words, this was the holy book made visual and physical: by walking through a door in a city on earth, an ordinary believer could step into the realm of God. As Napoleon apparently said, on his first visit to Chartres Cathedral, 'Here an atheist would feel uneasy.'

The Chartres labyrinth is still the object of fascination. Even though it has no walls, it provides a challenge that is hard to resist, and adds a further dimension of mystery and wonder to the cathedral.

Calm sea, low sky, an eternity of sand lined by grass-tufted dunes — there is little to suggest the tumult that erupted here in June 1944, and the memories that have rendered this landscape forever sacred.

OMAHA BEACH

Latitude 49°22'N **Longitude** 0°53'W	
Location Normandy, northwest France	
Faith None	
Built From 1944	
Approximate area 12 square kilometres (5 sq miles)	
Access Cemetery open daily, during normal working hours	

There's a profound stillness now at the Normandy American Cemetery and Memorial at Colleville-sur-Mer. Neat ranks of crosses and stars of David fan out across the manicured lawns. A large reflecting pool mirrors the sky. The trees sigh in the sea breezes. Seagulls mew overhead. Views out across the grassy dunes lead to the long beach lapped by the sea to its impassive, timeless rhythm.

Down below, on the sands where many of these men died, the atmosphere is barely less sombre and sacred. Many battlefields have a certain sanctity to them; at Omaha Beach it derives, ultimately, from the knowledge that much blood was spilled on this wet shore – the blood mostly of very young men fighting a decisive engagement in a grand and deeply righteous cause, the liberation of Europe from Nazi occupation.

At dawn on 6 June 1944, the German troops manning the fortifications on the chalk cliffs suddenly found themselves the target of a massive naval bombardment from Allied cruisers and destroyers. The sky above throbbed to the drone of 450 aircraft, which unloaded tonnes of bombs to their rear. Then the horizon filled with hundreds of landing craft, powering their way through rough seas towards the beach.

This was D-Day, the opening gambit of Operation Overlord, the Allied invasion of Normandy – and the first step in the march on Berlin to end the Second World War. The largest ever amphibian assault aimed to land 130,000 US, British and Canadian troops along an 80-kilometre (50-mile) front on the coast of Normandy. This particular sector of coast, codenamed Omaha, had been assigned to the Americans, mainly the 29th and 1st Infantry Divisions and three companies of US Army Rangers. They had spent months training in southwest England under a blanket of secrecy. Now the day

TRAVELLER'S TIPS

Best time to go: Any time of year. The summer months have more pleasant weather, but will be busier during school holidays (July–August).

Look out for: The Normandy American Cemetery and Memorial at Colleville-sur-Mer has a visitor centre that presents details of Operation Overlord and the events at Omaha Beach.

Dos and don'ts: For a fuller picture of the background to the Normandy campaign and the Battle for Caen, visit the Mémorial de Caen, which is 50 kilometres (31 miles) to the southeast.

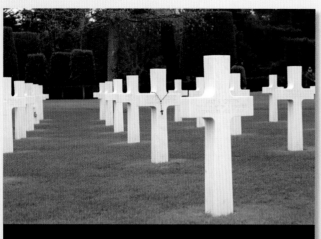

The US Army made a temporary cemetery at Colleville-sur-Mer two days after the landings. After the war, the Normandy American Cemetery was created close by; it contains the remains of 9,387 American military dead. Most of these died in the Normandy landings and in ensuing engagements, but some were losses from earlier air action. Walls of the Missing are inscribed with a further 1,557 names.

had come. But nothing went to plan. Foul weather had forced the Allied Command to postpone the attack for a day, and still the sea was rough. Because of the cloud cover, the bombers fractionally delayed releasing their bombs for fear of hitting their own troops: instead of decimating and disabling the coastal defences, they fell uselessly on fields and villages in the hinterland. The beach defences were stronger than expected, reinforced with Czech hedgehogs (anti-tank obstacles), metal gates and booby traps. Amphibious tanks, which were supposed to land and provide cover, sank out to sea or were knocked out by artillery.

The infantry, many of them disorientated by seasickness, disembarked under heavy fire to wade in to the shore, burdened by their kit and weapons. Many drowned; many were machine-gunned in their landing crafts as soon as the ramp dropped. Those that reached the shore then faced the 300 metres (330 yards) of open sand exposed by the low tide. Ahead lay a 45-metre (150-ft) curtain of 'bluffs' that had to be scaled to outflank and quell the enemy guns hidden in their reinforced-concrete bunkers.

Within a few hours, small parties of rangers and infantrymen succeeded in reaching the base of the cliffs, and then climbing up the steep paths to work their way around the fortifications. German reinforcements had been diverted to other sectors of coast, where defences had been penetrated by British, Canadian and other US troops. By nightfall the Americans had secured their beachhead.

It was a victory. But of all the D-Day landings this had been the most brutal confrontation: 1,000 Americans died on the beach, and perhaps a total of 5,000 Americans had been killed, wounded or missing. The Germans suffered 1,200 casualties. Those young lives are remembered today with moving dignity at the American Military Cemetery, and by all those who walk the broad, quiet sands that still bear that codename in their honour.

Anilore Banon's sculpture called 'Les Braves' was commissioned by the French government to mark the 60th anniversary of the landings in 2004. Lapped by the tide, it forms a kind of triptych representing the Wings of Hope, the Rise of Freedom and the Wings of Fraternity.

LASCAUX

Latitude 42°02'N **Longitude** 1°10'E	
Location Dordogne, southwest France	
Faith Prehistoric	
Age About 17,000 years	
Approximate area 430 square metres (4,630 sq ft)	
Access Original inaccessible; ticketed access to the replica	

Neat, cut-stone steps lead down to a door set in the hillside, but the door is firmly locked. Beyond it, tantalizingly, lies one of the world's most precious art treasures: an underground gallery with walls and ceilings covered with paintings and engravings some 17,000 years old. Soon after it was first discovered in 1940 by four local teenage boys and their dog, it became known as 'The Sistine Chapel of Prehistoric Art'.

The Lascaux cave is alive with animals – cattle, horses, deer, pictured with extraordinary dynamism and skill, running, overlapping, some huge, some tiny, some just silhouettes scratched into the soft limestone walls. Many of the animals pictured are extinct: aurochs (a kind of wild cattle); the elk-like megaloceros; rhinoceros present in Ice Age Europe; the mysterious deer with two long, straight horns, nicknamed 'the unicorn' but never identified.

What went on here? There is an intensity in the images that suggests they are more than mere decoration. There is no sign of habitation. Was this a place of ritual – of shamanistic ceremonies designed to influence the success of semi-nomadic hunters? Or cosmological charts, mapping the heavens in constellations? We can only guess and wonder.

Lascaux cave has been closed to the public since 1963 after exposure to the heat and carbon dioxide of many thousands of enraptured visitors was shown to be damaging the paintings. A faithful replica of key parts of the caves, called Lascaux II, was opened in 1983, just 200 metres (650 ft) away. Today only the scientists are allowed rare access to the mysterious wonder that provides a unique bridge through art to our forebears.

Lascaux II enables visitors to experience the wonders of the original cave, including the impressive 'Great Hall of the Bulls'.

LOURDES

Latitude 43°06'N **Longitude** 0°03'W	
Location Hautes-Pyrénées, southwest France	
Faith Christian (Roman Catholic)	
Age 150 years	
Approximate area 37 square kilometres (14 sq miles)	
Access Free, open access to almost all the sites, 24 hours a day	

Until 1858, Lourdes was an unremarkable market town lying in the foothills of the Pyrenees. Then between February and July of that year 14-year-old Bernadette Soubirous – daughter of a laundress and an out-of-work miller – had a series of 18 visions of the Virgin Mary at the entrance of a cave overlooking the River Gave de Pau. Today, Lourdes is the world's most visited healing pilgrimage site, attracting some 25,000 visitors a day during the season (Easter to October), and 5 million a year.

On 11 February 1858, returning home from firewood-collecting, Bernadette heard a rush of wind and saw the apparition for the first time: a beautiful girl, bathed in a soft light and dressed in white robes. Over the next few days, when she returned to the site accompanied by her sisters and friends, she – and she alone – saw and heard the same vision. Word spread in the town, causing a sensation and dividing opinion. Many thought that she was suffering some kind of psychotic delusions, or simply testing their gullibility.

Under questioning, she remained resolute and calm in her testimony. She resisted the suggestion that she was seeing a vision of the Virgin Mary, referring to her instead simply as *Aqueró*, meaning 'that one' in the local Occitan language. On 25 February, in a trance, Bernadette began drinking water from the floor of the cave, smearing her face with mud. Surely this was madness! But she later revealed that *Aqueró* had told her to 'drink and wash in the spring'; her followers dug in the cave and, true enough, uncovered a spring. Within days, several miracle cures had been attributed to the spring water.

The Sanctuary rises to a crescendo with the spires and dome of the Rosary Basilica, surmounted by a gilded crown and cross donated in 1924 by Ireland; Our Lady of the Immaculate Conception soars behind.

Eventually, on 25 March, the apparition revealed to Bernadette that she was the 'Immaculate Conception'. It was a turning point for the Church: this was a term for the Virgin Mary that had only recently been sanctioned by the Pope – and one that local people, let alone Bernadette, would not normally have known.

But by now Lourdes was in turmoil, and arousing the interest of the national press. A number of other girls began to experience visions. Panicked, the authorities closed off the cave. On 16 July Bernadette saw her final vision from across the river, and then she declared that her work was done. To escape her celebrity, she went to work at the hospice of the Sisters of Charity of Nevers in Lourdes; and at the age of 22, she moved to the mother house at Nevers in Burgundy to train as a nun. Here she died of tuberculosis in 1879, aged just 35. She was eventually formally declared a saint in 1933, and her preserved body, at Nevers, is itself a focus of pilgrimage.

Here the famous statue of the Virgin Mary that stands over the sacred cave is replicated on a pilgrimage banner. Pilgrims visit the cave, called the Grotte de Massabielle, to touch the walls, and drink and bathe in the spring water.

Back at Lourdes, two large churches – the neo-Gothic Basilica of Our Lady of the Immaculate Conception (1876) and the neo-Byzantine Basilica of Our Lady of the Rosary (1889) – were built on the hill above the cave. At first it was the visions that drew the pilgrims, but as stories of the miraculous healing power of the springs began to spread, this became the main focus.

Tens of thousands of ill and disabled believers now go to Lourdes every year, accompanied by volunteer helpers. 'Immediate and permanent' miracle cures have been reported over the years – some 70 of these verified as otherwise inexplicable by the rigorously investigative Lourdes Medical Bureau, which was established by the Church. But the Church is anxious not to arouse false hopes. Lourdes is about spiritual as well as physical healing: a deep sense of consolation is delivered by the humbling experience of a community travelling and working together towards a common purpose.

TRAVELLER'S TIPS

Best time to go: Lourdes is open all year, but the main season (with processions) runs from Palm Sunday (just before Easter) to late October. The busiest times are Easter and August.

Look out for: 'In the Footsteps of St Bernadette', a walk over 1.7 kilometres (1 mile), which links several sites of her life, such as her birthplace (the mill) and modest childhood home.

Dos and don'ts: Be patient. At busy times you have to be prepared to wait in queues for at least an hour to visit the cave, or the baths.

Pilgrim groups leave their wooden crosses around the crucifix in the Espanade as mementoes of their sense of achievement and community.

VATICAN CITY

Latitude 41°54'N **Longitude** 12°27'E	
Location Rome, Italy	
Faith Christian (Roman Catholic)	
Age First church AD 326; independent city-state from 1929	
Approximate area 44 hectares (109 acres)	
Access Free access to St Peter's; ticketed entry to museums	

Urbi et Orbi is the name of the potent blessing issued by the Pope at Easter and Christmas from the balcony in the façade of St Peter's Basilica, at the heart of the Vatican – a prayer that offers conditional remission of sins to the huge, rapturous crowds of the faithful gathered in St Peter's Square below. Usually translated as 'To the City and to the World', it is an apt description, for the Vatican City – a walled enclave just to the west of the centre of Rome, and the world's smallest independent state – is the supreme headquarters of the Roman Catholic Church, whose reach encompasses the globe.

A term originally used by the Ancient Romans to preface public proclamations, *Urbi et Orbi* is just one of countless vestiges of a continuous history that stretches right back to the time of Christ. St Peter's Basilica stands over what is believed to be the tomb of the Apostle St Peter himself. Tradition holds that he was martyred in around AD 64 in an adjacent stadium called the Circus of Nero – crucified head-down at his own

request, so as not to emulate Christ. The Ancient Egyptian obelisk that now stands in the middle of St Peter's Square, transported to Rome at the orders of Emperor Caligula in AD 37, would have witnessed the scene.

This direct link to one of Christ's closest associates, in his final test of faith, confers a powerful sanctity to the site. Nearly 2,000 years of history and tradition, and vast wealth, have transformed the Vatican City into a phenomenal concentration of art and architecture that may sometimes obscure this sanctity – but it is unmistakeable when pilgrims gather here in their tens of thousands to celebrate the big festivals of the Christian calendar.

St Peter's Basilica is an eloquent symbol of the power and status of the Roman Catholic Church. The earliest church here was begun by Constantine, the first Christian Roman Emperor, in AD 326. By the 15th century, it had fallen into

TRAVELLER'S **TIPS**

Best time to go: Any time of year. Easter is a high point in the calendar. Museums are closed most Sundays, and on Christian holidays. Go early in the day to avoid crowds.

Look out for: In St Peter's Basilica, an elevator ascends to a gallery inside the dome, where views over Rome can be seen from the roof; then 320 steps lead up to the lantern that crowns the dome.

Dos and don'ts: Do observe the dress code, which is strictly enforced and applies to men and women: no shorts, bare shoulders or miniskirts – even on a hot day.

Four thousand years of history are caught in a glance across St Peter's Square, with the ancient Egyptian obelisk standing close to the site where St Peter was martyred.

disrepair and plans were hatched to replace it. Construction eventually began in 1505, just as Rome was becoming a pole of the High Renaissance, but it took 120 years to complete it. The original design was the work of Donato Bramante; Michelangelo followed, and was responsible for the dome. Bernini took up the reins in the 17th century, adding richly ornate Baroque flourishes. Outside, his monumental, sweeping arcades flank St Peter's Square with their 284 columns. The vast interior of the basilica is a sumptuous confection of marble inlay, mosaics, statuary and the elaborate tombs of various popes. Here too is Michelangelo's extraordinary masterpiece, the *Pietà*, depicting the crucified Christ lying in the lap of his mother Mary – a supreme expression of human suffering and Christian compassion.

As the wealthy rulers of extensive territories, as well as leaders of an international Church, the popes were patrons of the arts, notably during the Renaissance. Their former apartments in the Vatican now contain a dozen museums of astonishing richness, with about 7 kilometres (4.3 miles) of galleries in all. Most celebrated of all are the Raphael Rooms – a suite of rooms decorated with murals by Raphael and his workshop – and the Sistine Chapel, with its famous ceiling painted by Michelangelo in 1508–12.

Vatican City is far from a museum piece: this is an active centre of administration and government. Even the Sistine Chapel still serves its historic function: this is where the conclave of cardinals meets to elect a new pope. Small furnaces link it to a chimney that signals – with a puff of white smoke – to the crowds massed in St Peter's Square outside that a decision has been reached about who will be the next successor to the Holy See of St Peter.

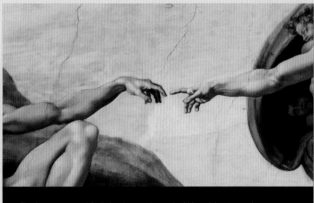

The famous image of God's hand giving the spark of life to Adam lies at the centre of the Sistine Chapel ceiling. Nine scenes from the Book of Genesis, plus images of prophets and biblical scenes, fill the ceiling over a chapel the size of two tennis courts.

Like 'the maternal arms of Mother Church' is how Bernini described St Peter's Square, with its many columns and statues of saints.

Sturdy like a Viking ship, the church centres
upon four strong vertical posts, the staves;
they form the basic square of the soaring nave,
elaborated with the aisles and belltower.

Latitude 61°2'N **Longitude** 7°48'E	
Location Sognefjord area, central southern Norway	
Faith Christian (not active)	
Built c.1180–1250	
Approximate area 60 square metres (646 sq ft)	
Access Ticketed entry, May to September only, daily	

BORGUND STAVE CHURCH

Woodwork, especially woodwork fashioned many generations ago, has an especially evocative appeal: its smell, its touch, its warmth, its patina of age. And wooden buildings have a human scale. The medieval wooden stave churches of Norway speak of a communal and personal relationship with God. Of all the 29 that have miraculously survived fire, rot, neglect and misdemeanour, the stave church of Borgund is the most extraordinary and the most enchanting.

The stave churches of Norway were built at the end of the Viking era, after the Norwegians, with considerable reluctance, had accepted the Christianity forced upon them by their kings, notably St Olaf (reigned 1015–28). The earliest surviving stave church dates from 1130; Borgund was built after 1180. Inside, it has been kept simple, with decorative flourishes seen only in the line of carved x-shapes of the cross of St Andrew (to whom the church is dedicated) at an upper level; the sympathetic altar piece, depicting the crucifixion, was painted in 1654. There are no pews. Congregations would stand for the services, men and boys to the right, women and girls to the left.

The many-tiered roofs are tiled with timber shingles right up the belltower at the tip. The four upper roof finials are highly stylized dragon's heads – recalling the figureheads of the Viking longships, and the close proximity of a pagan past. The building has not been used regularly as a church since 1868, and has been owned by the Society for the Preservation of Norwegian Ancient Monuments since 1877. But that does not diminish the aura of precious sanctity that the timbers seem to exude.

TRAVELLER'S TIPS

Best time to go: Summer. The church looks pretty in the snow in winter but is generally closed. Occasional services are held in the church (for example, for Easter).

Look out for: The main door is surrounded by intricate carving that echoes Viking themes: entwined and fighting snakes and dragons and other animal motifs, and acanthus foliage.

Dos and don'ts: Make time to see the Visitor Centre, which has details about other local stave churches, notably at Urnes (the oldest, 1130) and Hopperstad (c.1140).

SANTIAGO DE COMPOSTELA

At the top of the Monte do Gozo ('Hill of Joy'), two statues of pilgrim-monks wave their arms to greet their first sight of their goal, the cathedral of Santiago de Compostela. This is the very last hill on the Camino Francés (French Road), along which, for more than 1,000 years, pilgrims in their millions have come, from all over Europe and beyond.

Santiago de Compostela is Christianity's third most important pilgrimage destination, after Jerusalem and Rome. It reached the height of its fame and popularity in the early Middle Ages, but quietened down after the Black Death ravaged Europe in the mid-14th century, and after the Protestant Reformation in the 16th.

Since the Second World War there has been a resurgence, and now some 200,000 pilgrims make their way to the city each year, on foot or on bicycles, along the same old paths and roads that cross northern Spain from the Pyrenees, staying in the simple hostels and refuges that lie along the way. Many come out of religious conviction. Others come for vaguer reasons: the camaraderie, journeying with a purpose along a historical path through beautiful countryside, to find themselves. And, one way or another, many find this a profound spiritual experience.

The cathedral is the centrepoint of the city and the main focus of pilgrimage. Its frothy baroque spires stand out in marked contrast to the coolly secular buildings that flank it, and face onto the huge Praza do Obradoiro.

Latitude 42°52'N **Longitude** 8°32'W

Location Galicia, northwest Spain

Faith Christian (Roman Catholic)

Built From AD 829

Approximate area 220 square kilometres (85 sq miles)

Access Free access to the cathedral, open daily

The story behind the fame of Santiago de Compostela is based entirely on legend. At the heart of it is St James the Greater, the fisherman, one of Christ's 12 disciples. After Christ's crucifixion, he is said to have come to Roman Spain to evangelize. The Bible says he was killed by Herod (Agrippa) 'with the sword' – which is taken to indicate that St James was beheaded in Jerusalem in AD 44. Legend says his body was then carried by two disciples (or angels) to Jaffa, where they set sail in a rudderless boat to see where providence would take them. They ended up at Padrón on the coast of Galicia, where St James (Santiago in Spanish) was buried. Eight centuries later a hermit called Pelagius (locally, Pelayo) dreamed of guiding stars, which led him (or the local bishop, Theomodir) to the grave in the 'Field of Stars' – Compostela. In 829 King Alfonso II of Asturias built a chapel on the site (where the cathedral now stands) to house the relics, and soon this started to attract the first pilgrims.

This was a time when the Muslim Moors occupied most of Spain. The long Christian struggle to reconquer Spain, the Reconquista, began in the north. Legend again calls in St James who was said to have appeared to lead the Spanish to victory in the Battle of Clavijo (which supposedly took place in 834). Thereafter, Santiago Matamoros (St James, Slayer of the Moors) became the patron saint of the Reconquista, and the battle cry. And he remains Spain's patron saint to this day.

Meanwhile Santiago de Compostela grew rich on pilgrimage, developing into one of Spain's most attractive cities, and packed with churches, monasteries, hostels and hospices, as well as the mansions and palaces of the rich and powerful.

But the centrepiece remains the cathedral, where the supposed bones of St James lie in a silver casket in the crypt beneath the altar. The cathedral was built in grand Romanesque style in 1075–1122, but has been added to over the centuries. In a ritual of uncertain origin, pilgrims place their fingers in five holes near the base of the Pórtico on their way to receive their certificate of indulgence called a Compostela. The façade bearing three soaring Baroque towers, with a statue of James in the middle, now stands in front of the Pórtico, dominating the city. And it is the first, distant sight of these that makes pilgrims cry out in rapture as they crest the Monte do Gozo.

A distant view from the north, from the Miradoiro do Monte de Deus, shows the spires of the cathedral rising unchallenged above the skyline of St James's city.

A statue of St James takes centre stage high on the façade of the cathedral, dating from the rebuilding in Baroque style in 1740. He is seen carrying his staff and bearing scallop shells on his chest and the broad brim of his hat. Scallop shells are used to mark the multiple pilgrimage routes leading to Santiago de Compostela from across Europe – called collectively the Way of St James (El Camino de Santiago).

LA MEZQUITA DE CÓRDOBA

Latitude 37°52'N **Longitude** 4°46'W	
Location Córdoba, Andalucía, southern Spain	
Faith Christian (Roman Catholic)	
Built AD 784–18th century	
Approximate area 21,000 square metres (226,000 sq ft)	
Access Daily, ticketed after 10 a.m.	

A view from the 14th-century Calahorra Tower and Roman Bridge across the River Guadalquivir shows La Mezquita looming over the city at the far end.

From the air, this is perplexing. At the centre of Córdoba, a church appears to be sinking into the middle of a large rectangular field, neatly ploughed into broad, straight furrows. One end of the field is filled with what looks like a long swimming pool, but green, overlooked by an isolated, wedding-cake tower.

The reality on the ground is every bit as contradictory. Here in Spain is one of Islam's greatest and most extraordinary pieces of architecture: a mosque built over two centuries, beginning in AD 784. Inside is a strange, disorientating and dingy forest of 856 columns topped by two tiers of stripy horseshoe and semicircular arches in red brick and stone, beneath a painted timber roof. But in the midst of it rises a bright 16th-century cathedral – Gothic, Plateresque, Renaissance and Baroque, full of exuberant bravado and flourish.

Although this complex has served as the cathedral of Córdoba since the Christian conquest of the Moors in 1236, it is still known locally as La Mezquita, Spanish for 'The Mosque' – a measure for the affection in which the original mosque is still held. It was a wonder even in own day. When the young Umayyad prince Abd al-Rahman fled the bloody Abbasid Revolution in Damascus in AD 750, he came to Moorish Andalucía and founded a new emirate, with Córdoba as his

TRAVELLER'S **TIPS**

Best time to go: Any time of year, but summer in southern Spain can be very hot. To avoid the crowds, go early in the day (before 10 a.m.), or arrive an hour or so before closing time at 7 p.m.

Look out for: The tenth-century *mihrab* is a jewel of Moorish Islamic architecture and decoration, with interlacing arches beneath a scalloped dome, which is covered in Byzantine mosaics.

Dos and don'ts: Be aware that there is much controversy over whether Muslims should be allowed to pray in this 'mosque-cathedral'. Currently this is forbidden.

capital. He wanted to build a Great Mosque as a prestigious religious centre at the heart of his kingdom, and adopted the site of an old Visigothic Christian church.

The many-coloured columns – marble, granite, onyx, jasper – were salvaged from Roman and Visigothic ruins, and dictated the structure. These being relatively small, height could be gained only through arches stacked in two layers – an innovation at the time. More aisles were added in blocks by Abd al-Rahman's successors in four stages, to achieve the

The use of multiple ranks of columns is a familiar style in Islamic architecture, giving rise to the term 'forest mosques', often used in Turkey. But the sheer number of columns – 856 in all – set La Mezquita apart in scale and beauty. The design has been called the architectural equivalent of a mantra, repeated rhythmically countless times to liberate the mind and set it on a higher plain.

present colossal proportions: an interior space the size of two soccer pitches. It was the second largest mosque in all Islam, after Mecca.

In the meantime, Córdoba had become Europe's most glittering city, fuelled by trade and crafts – a city of palaces and mosques, libraries, medical schools and universities. Muslims, Jews and Christians flourished in a society noted for its tolerance. Its scholarship and learning were a foundation block of the later European Renaissance.

Decline set in during the 11th century, and Córdoba never recovered its illustrious status after it fell to the Christian Reconquista in 1236. For a while the mosque remained more or less intact, apart from some *mudéjar* (Moorish-influenced) additions, including two exquisite 14th-century chapels; and the minaret was converted into a belltower. In the 1520s, however, the Church authorities campaigned to impose a more Christian stamp on the building. So rose the cathedral in the midst of all the columns. Although impressive in its own right, and – structurally – seamlessly joined to the great hall of arches, it is a jarring intrusion. This is not a modern judgement. King Charles V, who had approved the plan, declared, 'They have destroyed something unique in the world, and have put in its place something that can been seen anywhere.'

Today, to appreciate the genius of the original mosque, you have to picture how it looked in the Moorish golden age. From the busy souk, you entered through an elaborate, arched doorway into an open, arcaded courtyard, filled with ranks of orange trees and palms (that green swimming pool). From here, you passed through one of the many high, open arches – now mostly filled in – that led to the 19 interior aisles and flooded them with light. The mosque offered a natural progression from busy city life to an oasis of living trees and then into a cool forest of stone, and to prayer before the sumptuous *mihrab*, in the direction of Mecca.

The 16th-century cathedral rises up from the midst of the mosque, while the belltower beyond stands on the site of the old minaret, as its name Torre de Alminar acknowledges.

FÁTIMA

'If you come simply as a visitor, respect the pilgrims at prayer. This place has nothing to satisfy mere curiosity. What matters here is the heart.' So reads an official notice at Fátima, one of the world's great Marian shrines, where pilgrims from around the world come to venerate the Virgin Mary. Two large churches bookend a vast esplanade: the Basilica of Our Lady of the Rosary, built 1928–53, and the huge and ultra-modern, circular Church of the Most Holy Trinity, completed in 2007. They host the hundreds of thousands of pilgrims, and provide a setting for the passionate outpourings of devotion on two days in the middle of each month between May and October, when the revered statue of Our Lady of Fátima, bearing her outsized golden crown, is carried through the esplanade on a flower-bedecked pallet.

The story of Fátima dates back to 1916, during the First World War, when three young shepherd children from the little village of Fátima – Lúcia Santos (aged ten) and her siblings Francisco (nine) and Jacinta (seven) Marto – were visited three times by an angel imploring them to pray in order to bring peace to the world. The following year, on 13 May 1917, the Virgin Mary appeared before them near an oak tree in a meadow hollow called Cova da Iria. 'We were

Os puros de coração verão a Deus

PORTUGAL
SPAIN
Fátima

Latitude 37°35'N **Longitude** 8°38'W	
Location Beira Litoral, west central Portugal	
Faith Christian (Roman Catholic)	
Built From 1928	
Approximate area 15 hectares (37 acres)	
Access Free access to the churches	

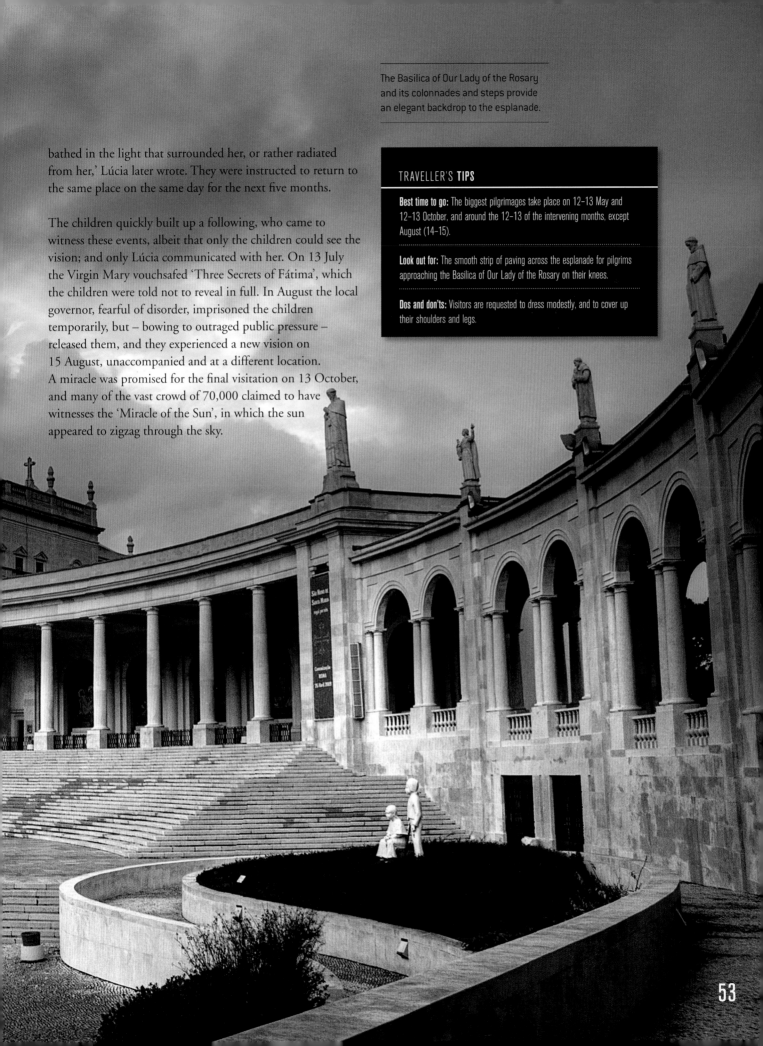

The Basilica of Our Lady of the Rosary and its colonnades and steps provide an elegant backdrop to the esplanade.

bathed in the light that surrounded her, or rather radiated from her,' Lúcia later wrote. They were instructed to return to the same place on the same day for the next five months.

The children quickly built up a following, who came to witness these events, albeit that only the children could see the vision; and only Lúcia communicated with her. On 13 July the Virgin Mary vouchsafed 'Three Secrets of Fátima', which the children were told not to reveal in full. In August the local governor, fearful of disorder, imprisoned the children temporarily, but – bowing to outraged public pressure – released them, and they experienced a new vision on 15 August, unaccompanied and at a different location. A miracle was promised for the final visitation on 13 October, and many of the vast crowd of 70,000 claimed to have witnesses the 'Miracle of the Sun', in which the sun appeared to zigzag through the sky.

TRAVELLER'S TIPS

Best time to go: The biggest pilgrimages take place on 12–13 May and 12–13 October, and around the 12–13 of the intervening months, except August (14–15).

Look out for: The smooth strip of paving across the esplanade for pilgrims approaching the Basilica of Our Lady of the Rosary on their knees.

Dos and don'ts: Visitors are requested to dress modestly, and to cover up their shoulders and legs.

Fátima became the focus of Marian devotion; a little Chapel of the Apparitions was built over the main site of the visions (now encased in a glass building on the esplanade). Apparently, in the second apparition the Virgin Mary said that she would 'take Francisco and Jacinta soon'. They fell victim to the Spanish flu epidemic and died in 1919 and 1920 respectively. Lúcia, the main source of the account, lived on, and had further visions in the 1920s. She became a Carmelite nun, and died aged 97 in 2005.

The 'Three Secrets of Fátima' have been revealed by the Roman Catholic Church only after their arcanely worded predictions appear to have matched events. The first two, involving the two World Wars and the dangers posed by a godless Russia, were revealed in 1941. The fall of Soviet Communism was later linked to the visions. On 13 May 1991 Pope John Paul II mysteriously placed the bullet that nearly killed him in an assassination attempt – exactly ten years before – in the crown of the statue of the Virgin Mary at Fátima. In 2000 the third secret was revealed – and was interpreted as a prediction of that assassination attempt.

Officially, the Roman Catholic Church has always treated the events of Fátima with reserve. Nonetheless, Fátima has attracted the devotion of several popes, notably Pope John Paul II and Benedict XVI. And many millions of ordinary believers. Every year they bring to Our Lady of Fátima their devotion – and their hearts.

Figurines of the crowned Virgin Mary, Pope John Paul II, Jesus Christ, saints and the bespectacled Lúcia of Fátima, in her nun's outfit, provide treasured mementoes for pilgrims. As with all pilgrimage sites, devotion also brings commercial opportunities, and providing for the needs of the 4–5 million visitors who come to Fátima each year has had a transformational effect on the local economy.

For much of the year Fátima stands silent, as if in anticipation of the throngs of people who converge on it during the high points of the summer pilgrimage season.

The monastery of Simonos Petras, founded in 1257, has perhaps the most spectacular setting of all, set on a high plinth of rock overlooking the Aegean Sea. The monks work the terraced gardens that cascade down the mountain.

MOUNT ATHOS

Latitude 49°9'N **Longitude** 24°19'E	
Location Macedonia, northern Greece	
Faith Christian (Eastern Orthodox)	
Built From AD 963	
Approximate area 335 square kilometres (130 sq miles)	
Access By ferry from Ouranoupolis. Restricted to males over 18 equipped with a visa obtained in advance	

The best-known fact about Mount Athos is that women are not allowed. With rare exceptions, they have not been allowed for more than 1,000 years. The population of some 2,000 Eastern Orthodox monks and their lay assistants are all male, and all over the age of 18. The monks are careful to explain this not as some kind of misogyny but as part of their self-sacrifice: they know their mortal weaknesses, and they want to be able to dedicate their lives utterly to God.

Mount Athos is really a peninsula 50 kilometres (31 miles) long and 12 kilometres (7.5 miles) wide, pointing southward from the Macedonian mainland of Greece into the northernmost extremes of the Aegean Sea. It is called Mount Athos for its conical, often snow-capped mountain at the southern tip, named after the giant Athos of Greek myth. In Greece, the mountain and the peninsula are referred to simply as Agion Oros ('Holy Mountain').

The rest of the peninsula rises steeply to a hilly ridge covered with chestnut and pine forest, and is rimmed by a rocky coastline. Dotted all around the coast, and sprinkled here and there inland, are 20 large Orthodox monasteries. Many of them are huge, like small towns, or fortresses or palaces, recalling the heyday of Mount Athos, in the early 1900s, when there were 7,000 resident monks on the peninsula. Richly endowed, favoured over the centuries by foreign potentates of the Eastern Orthodox family – Greek, Russian, Serbian, Romanian, Bulgarian – many are also richly decorated with frescoes and mosaics and have collections of priceless manuscripts and sacred icons.

But this is no life of luxury. The monks – who now come from all over the world – lead austere lives of prayer and work. The day begins at 3 a.m., roused from just three hours' sleep by a mallet struck against a timber plank (a tradition pre-dating the arrival of bells) to begin eight hours of daily church services. They eat twice a day, in silence, for ten minutes.

And when they are not at services, the monks work. They may help to run the monasteries, or work in the fields and olive groves, or as fishermen, mechanics, taxi-drivers, icon-painters, tailors. Even then they are at prayer, constantly pleading for the mercy of Jesus. They wear black, they say, as a symbol of death. They are dead to the world, and they embrace death as the opportunity to be with their Saviour. Their bodies will be buried, and then later the bones exhumed to be piled up with those of their brethren in the ossuaries.

The monks can leave Mount Athos, but most rarely do so. That said, they are not isolated. Some 35,000 pilgrims come to the peninsula every year. All of them are male, of course; they have to have a special visa, which is granted only on application well in advance. Typically, a visa lasts for three nights, during which a pilgrim can move from one monastery to another, lodged and fed for free, but longer stays may be granted. All of this is policed by a self-governing administration run by the Holy Community – the world's longest continually functioning parliament – in the small, inland capital called Karyes.

Pilgrims come to absorb some of the profound piety of Mount Athos, and to escape into a world that is virtually untouched by the hectic demands of modern technology. Legend has it that the Virgin Mary arrived at Mount Athos when her ship was blown off course during a storm. As she expressed her admiration for its beauty, she heard the voice of her son say: 'Let this place be your inheritance and your garden, a paradise and a haven of salvation for those seeking to be saved.' It is undoubtedly a haven for those seeking to be saved, but exclusively for men – in honour, they say, of their devotion to the Virgin Mary.

TRAVELLER'S TIPS

Best time to go: Any time of year. Spring (March–May) is especially attractive, when the weather is often sunny and the landscape is speckled with wild flowers. Summer can be extremely hot.

Look out for: Clocks following the Byzantine time system, where the new day begins at sunset. Note also that the Julian calendar is still used here, 13 days behind the rest of the world.

Dos and don'ts: Don't expect to reach Mount Athos without a visa; you will be turned away. Expect to do plenty of walking.

The Iviron Monastery was founded by Georgian monks in the tenth century, and is noted for its exceptional library of more than 20,000 books and manuscripts. It houses about 30 working monks and novices.

PARTHENON

Although created some 2,500 years ago, and shattered by neglect, war and pillaging, the Parthenon still ranks as one of the world's most majestic buildings, and a model of perfection in architectural design.

Set high above the city of Athens, on the rocky plinth called the Acropolis, the Parthenon was created first and foremost as an act of thanksgiving. In about 447 BC the architects Iktinos and Kallicrates, and the sculptor Phidias were brought together to produce the most magnificent shrine imaginable for Athena, the patron of the city and goddess of wisdom, inspiration and civilization, who was deemed to have rescued Athens from Persian invasion – a triumph that had ushered in a new Golden Age under the rule of Pericles.

The centrepiece of the building, in the closed sanctuary called the *naos*, was a colossal and costly statue of Athena Parthenos ('The Virgin'), constructed by Phidias out of ivory and gold. Beside the *naos* was a treasury for the recently formed alliance of Greek city-states called the Delian League. This core of two chambers was surrounded by an arcade of columns made of brilliant-white, fine-grained marble from the quarries of Mount Pentelikon, which lay 16 kilometres (10 miles) away.

It seems a simple enough plan, but in fact the success of the Parthenon depends on a number of subtle visual illusions. The columns, for instance, bulge towards the top to make them seem straight, compensating for the eye's tendency to make columns set in straight rows seem slightly concave. For similar reasons, they also lean slightly inwards. The corner columns are fatter than the others; otherwise they would have seemed thinner when seen in isolation against the sky. To achieve these effects, the component parts – such as the drums of stone that make up the columns – could not be mass-produced, but had to be individually fashioned, lending the building as a whole an organic character: production-line manufacture would have resulted in something altogether more coldly mechanical.

The Acropolis was a sacred precinct, strongly attached to the legends of the founding of Athens. Here Athena had defeated the sea god Poseidon in her bid to become the main patron of the city. The Acropolis, therefore, was her shrine, and contained a number of other monuments and temples dedicated to her. This included a huge bronze statue by Phidias of Athena Promachos ('Fighting on the Front Line'), whose gleaming spear was said to be visible out at sea 50 kilometres (30 miles) away.

Latitude 37°97'N **Longitude** 23°72'E	
Location Athens, Greece	
Faith Ancient Greek	
Built 447–432 BC	
Approximate area 2,147 square metres (23,117 sq ft)	
Access Open daily, tickets at the gate	

On its high plinth, the Parthenon always takes the limelight, especially when caught in the evening sun. It overshadows a string of other ancient wonders at ground level below, including the second-century AD Theatre of Herodes Atticus.

TRAVELLER'S **TIPS**

Best time to go: Any time of year. Summer can be very hot, so try to go early in the morning, or in the late afternoon. It's a 20-minute uphill walk to the Acropolis.

Look out for: The Belvedere at the eastern end of the Acropolis has famous panoramic views. On Sundays the Evzones (Presidential Guard in traditional costumes) raise and lower the Greek flag here.

Dos and don'ts: Don't miss the Acropolis Museum (it is at street level, just to the south). Opened in 2009, it displays numerous archaeological treasures in pristine modern galleries.

After the Romans conquered Greece in 146 BC, they maintained the sanctity of the Acropolis, adding their own temples and monuments. Thus the Parthenon survived more or less intact for about 700 years, until the Goths sacked the city in AD 267. In the fifth century, after the Roman Empire had become Christian, both the giant Athena statues were removed, and in the following century the Parthenon was converted into a Christian church. Later on, after Greece was conquered by the Ottoman Turks in 1458, it became a mosque.

In 1687, during a war with the Venetians, the Ottomans fortified the Acropolis and turned the Parthenon into a gunpowder magazine. It was hit by cannon fire and exploded, suffering catastrophic damage. In 1801–12, with the permission of the Ottoman rulers, the English Ambassador to Athens, the Earl of Elgin, carried off half of the sculptures; they were in turn purchased by the British Museum in London, where they still reside.

Even in its bombed-out and plundered form today, the Parthenon has an unsurpassed stately elegance. The original, however, was not only encrusted with sculpture, but also brightly painted.

What we see at the Parthenon today, therefore, are merely the broken ribs of the original. Yet it retains such poise and stately elegance that it is still inspires wonder and admiration – challenging the imagination to paint in what is missing. We may be remote from the religious beliefs and practices for which the Parthenon was built, but its genius still whispers to us across the millennia.

A fallen column at the Temple of Olympian Zeus, beneath the Parthenon (seen on its plinth to the rear), shows clearly how the fluted columns were made from drum-like blocks. Because of their tapering shape, each drum had to be made individually. The roughed-out blocks were hauled from the quarry, then shaped and trimmed on site. No mortar was used, so the drums had to be a perfect fit.

RUSSIA

Sergiyev Posad

Moscow

Latitude 58°18'N **Longitude** 38°08'E

Location Western Russia

Faith Russian Orthodox

Built 15th–18th centuries

Approximate area 10 hectares (25 acres)

Access Free access, throughout the year, from 8 a.m. to 6 p.m.

SERGIYEV POSAD

Imagine a cluster of huts surrounding a wooden chapel, deep in a remote forest in Western Russia, somewhere around the middle of the 14th century. It was in such a setting that one of Russia's most beloved saints, St Sergius (or Sergei) – famed for his humility, vow of poverty and service to others, and for his miracles – lived with his followers. They shared a simple life, close to nature, devoted to Christian contemplation. Sergei's family, originally of noble stock, farmed at nearby Radonezh, but as a young man in about 1344, he had retreated into the forest to live the life of a hermit. As his community grew around his little chapel dedicated to the Holy Trinity, he wrote a charter of rules of conduct in 1355, laying the foundations of Russian Orthodox monasticism.

At this time Russia had been under the yoke of the Mongols, or Tartars, for more than a century. Attracting growing respect as a holy man, Sergei helped to unite the Russian princes in revolt. Dmitri Donskoi, Prince of Moscow, came to him for a blessing before winning a decisive victory at the Battle of Kulikovo in 1380. Thereafter the Moscow princes, later the tsars, became patrons of his Trinity monastery – a royal connection set to become ever stronger over the centuries.

Saint Sergei died here in 1392, an old man in his 70s. In 1408 Tartar raiders destroyed his monastery, but in 1422

Winter cold enhances the beauty of Sergiyev Posad, but depletes the numbers of pilgrims, who usually throng the well to collect sacred water.

his successor, Saint Nikon, built a stone church here, the Cathedral of the Holy Trinity, in which the relics of Sergei were laid. The Tartars were finally defeated by Ivan the Terrible, Prince of Moscow and the first Tsar of all Russia, in the following century, and in 1559 he commissioned a second cathedral for the Trinity monastery to celebrate his victory: the Cathedral of the Assumption (or Dormition) of St Mary.

During the 17th century, the Trinity monastery was adorned by the best and most glorious Russian architecture, and the interior of the Cathedral of the Assumption was lavishly painted in 1684. In 1744, Empress Elizabeth of Russia – who made an annual pilgrimage here on foot from Moscow, a distance of 70 kilometres (43 miles) – bestowed upon the monastery the status of *lavra*, the highest rank among Russian Orthodox monasteries.

The Troitse-Sergiyeva Lavra soon became the wealthiest in all Russia. Topped by gilded and radiant blue onion domes, it took on a dream-like beauty, the soul and aspirations of the Russian Orthodox Church made manifest on earth.

But then came the godless years of Soviet Communism. After the Revolution of 1917, the authorities closed the monastery and strove to drain it of meaning – but they did not dare demolish it. In 1930 the surrounding city was renamed Zagorsk, after an obscure Bolshevik functionary called Vladimir Zagorksy. In 1945, however, the monastery was given back to the Church under carefully controlled conditions, and after the fall of Communism in 1991, the monastery was repopulated and finally restored to its full gilded, pastel-shaded glory. It now has some 300 resident monks and serves as the main seminary school of the Russian Orthodox Church, and as one of the residences of the Patriarch of Moscow.

The Troitse-Sergiyeva Lavra has once again become a place of pilgrimage, attracting many thousands of people throughout the year. They come to attend services in the 13 churches that are scattered across this spacious, tree-shaded enclave, to bask in the beauty of the 17th-century Baroque architecture of the monastery, and to admire the jewel-encrusted treasures on display in the old Vestry. They also come to drink the water from a sacred spring at the Chapel-at-the-Well, which is believed to effect cures – physically imbibing the essence of Russian Christianity and its hallowed bond to nationhood.

Sunshine glints on the golden onion domes of the Gateway Church of the Nativity of St John the Baptist. The aristocratic Stroganov family had it built at the very end of the 17th century.

At the end of the 17th century, at the instruction of Peter the Great, a new and very large refectory was built to accommodate the burgeoning numbers of monks, and was dedicated to St Sergei. Like virtually everything at Sergiyev Posad, it is visually captivating, with the outside walls painted with four-colour *trompe l'oeil* faceting, and garlands of vines around the columns.

CHURCH OF THE SAVIOUR ON THE SPILLED BLOOD

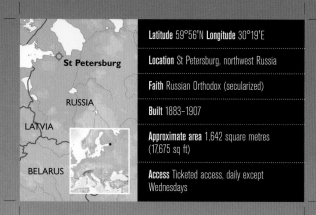

Latitude 59°56'N **Longitude** 30°19'E	
Location St Petersburg, northwest Russia	
Faith Russian Orthodox (secularized)	
Built 1883–1907	
Approximate area 1,642 square metres (17,675 sq ft)	
Access Ticketed access, daily except Wednesdays	

If ever a Fabergé Egg was turned into architecture, this might be the result. And just as the Fabergé workshops of St Petersburg fashioned their richly enamelled and bejewelled eggs for the imperial family, so too was this ornate and glittering church designed as an exclusive tribute to a tsar: Alexander II.

It marks the place in St Petersburg where his blood was spilled: the site of a bomb attack that led to his death in the Winter Palace a few hours later. Alexander II, aged 62, had already survived some seven assassination attempts. Notwithstanding, on 13 March 1881 he took his regular Sunday route to visit the military riding academy. On the embankments of the Griboedov Canal, at least three members of the republican anarchist group Narodnaya Volya (People's Will) were waiting. As his carriage passed, 20-year-old Nikolai Rysakov threw a grenade under the horses, killing a Cossack guard and wounding the driver. But the carriage was bombproof and Alexander survived. When he got out of the carriage to see what was happening, a second young anarchist, Ignaty Grinevitsky, threw another bomb, killing himself and blowing the legs off the Tsar.

Nothing about the exterior of the Church of the Saviour on the Spilled Blood would suggest the sombre tragedy that it commemorates. Rather, it is a confident statement of Russian national pride.

The interior of the church contrasts architecturally with the exterior, in that it consists of simple rectilinear columns, Romanesque arches and domes. But every single square inch is crammed with mosaics. Although reminiscent of the greatest Byzantine churches, the colour scheme is distinctively Russian in its floral pinks and yellows, and saturated blues and gold.

Alexander II had certainly made enemies in his politically volatile empire, exerting his autocratic powers to crush rebellion. But he was also a reformer and in 1861 he had overseen the abolition of serfdom – effectively a form of slavery. For this he earned the name 'Alexander the Liberator'. He had also been working on plans to introduce an elected government, the Duma, which may have provided a path towards constitutional monarchy and pricked the growing pressure for revolutionary change that erupted in 1917. Instead, his assassination reinforced the belief of his son Alexander III that Russia had to be ruled with an iron rod.

Alexander 'the Liberator' was not only admired by many of his subjects, being tsar also gave him a semi-religious status. The coronation ceremony underlined his position as God's selected ruler. So when Alexander III proposed that a church should be built on the site of the assassination, it was widely supported. Ambitious plans were hatched to create a magnificent church in traditional Russian style, with the kind of multicoloured onion domes seen on St Basil's Cathedral in Moscow (built in 1561), and in stark contrast to the more restrained neoclassical style of St Petersburg. All the interior surfaces, totalling more than 7,000 square metres (75,350 sq ft), were to be lined with mosaics made in the Byzantine style using small squares of tinted and gilded glass, arranged to form biblical scenes designed by many of the leading Russian artists of the day. Christ's Crucifixion is a key theme, inviting association with Alexander's own death.

The Cathedral of the Resurrection of Christ, as it was officially called, was finally consecrated in 1907. The cobblestones from the road where Alexander's blood had been spilled were carefully reinstated, under an elaborate canopy, and soon the 'Church of the Saviour on the Spilled Blood' became its popular name.

It was always more of a shrine than a church, and its public functions were limited to weekly requiems for the dead tsar. After the Communist Revolution of 1917, the church fell into decay; secularized in the 1930s, it was used as a vegetable store, and as a morgue during the Siege of Leningrad in 1941–4. Under Stalin, there was talk of demolishing it. Instead, in 1970, a massive 27-year restoration programme was initiated, and now the church is treated as a museum of mosaic art. It brings gasps of wonder from its many visitors for its sumptuous glamour. But the cobblestones also inspire meditative reflection: this is where a life was lost, and where the destiny of a nation may well have taken a fateful turn.

Night-time illuminations underline the fantastical conception of this church. The road now detours around the site where once it had led Tsar Alexander II straight on along the Griboedov Canal to his fate.

TEMPLE OF HEAVEN

This is where earth connected with heaven, where from 1420 to 1911 the Emperor of China – the 'Son of Heaven' – could exercise his unique power to communicate with the gods and, by performing intricate rituals and sacrifices faultlessly, ensure a good harvest for the coming year.

Twice a year, in spring and at the winter solstice, the Emperor made a grand procession from the Forbidden City to this temple complex 1.5 kilometres (1 mile) to the southeast, accompanied by his nobles, officials and guards, but hidden from the view of ordinary people. He would fast in the Temple of Abstinence, conduct rituals in the Imperial Vault of Heaven and the Hall of Prayer for Good Harvests, and make sacrifices on the open plinth of the Circular Mound Altar.

Originally built in 1406–20 by the Yongle Emperor, the third of the Ming Dynasty, the temple complex was designed in the image of Chinese cosmology, where heaven is round and earth is square. The Circular Mound Altar is surrounded by a square enclosure, as is the round and lavishly ornate Hall of Prayer for Good Harvests. Roofs are a deep, heavenly blue. The tiers of the platforms and roofs, balustrades and steps are composed in threes and nines – nine being the numerical symbol of heaven. The complex is aligned to the points of the compass, with gates to the north, east, south and west; the southern sector is enclosed by a square wall, and the more heavenly northern part by a higher semicircular wall.

With the collapse of the Qing dynasty and the end of imperial rule in 1912, the Temple of Heaven lost its ritual significance. It is now a public park, where thousands of Chinese come to spend their leisure time – and to wonder at the spiritual power that was once channelled through these sacred monuments.

Three sets of nine steps lead up to the round Temple of Heaven, with its three roofs. All numbers and shapes were propitious to ensure the best outcome for the Chinese emperors' ritual communion with the gods.

Latitude 39°52'N Longitude 116°24'E

Location Central Beijing

Faith Chinese Heaven worship

Built 1406–20, 1520, 1740

Approximate area 2.75 square kilometres
(1 sq mile)

Access Ticketed entry, year round

NORTH
KOREA

◇ Beijing

CHINA

WUDANG MOUNTAINS

Latitude 32°22'N **Longitude** 111°4'E	
Location Northern Hubei Province, China	
Faith Taoist	
Built From the 7th century AD	
Approximate area 250 square kilometres (96 sq miles)	
Access Ticketed entry to park, daily	

'Nature does not hurry, yet everything is accomplished.' This famous Taoist proverb sums up the central place that nature holds in Taoism, China's only major native-born religion. Nature is the guiding principle. Observe nature; be true to your own nature; for a balanced and harmonious life, aim to achieve no more than nature achieves.

The Wudang Mountains are sumptuously beautiful – a set of 72 sharply sculpted peaks and cloud-filled valleys draped with forests, glades, streams, waterfalls, pools. Taoists have been coming here to immerse themselves in nature, and meditate upon it, for more than 2,000 years.

For the original teachings, Taoists look back to the sage Lao Tzu, who is believed to have lived at the same time as Confucius in the sixth century BC. While Confucius provided guidelines for daily conduct, Lao Tzu – and the classic text ascribed to him, the *Tao Te Ching* – provided a spiritual framework for living. In origin, Taoism was not so much a religion as a philosophy: the Tao means simply 'The Way'. Nonetheless, it took on many of the aspects of a religion over time, with gods and legendary god-like characters, temples and monasteries.

The Taoists set up a series of temples, and shrines to natural features, in the Wudang Shan (Wudang Mountains). When the Chinese emperors in Beijing – some 1,000 kilometres (620 miles) to the northeast – adopted Taoism, they built a series of temples and palaces there, and the Wudang Mountains took on the gloss of high prestige. They also became a centre of learning, for philosophy, meditation, music, agriculture, herbal medicine – and the martial arts. Balance – reconciling the give-and-take of life, and the opposing yet complementary forces of yin and yang – is

Pilgrims who toil up the steep stone steps to the Wudang Mountains' precious shrine, the Golden Hall, are rewarded by spectacular views of jagged peaks and valleys.

TRAVELLER'S TIPS

Best time to go: For the most agreeable weather, and the best views, April–June or September–October (lovely autumnal colours).

Look out for: At the Nanyan Palace, the stone Dragon Head Incense Burner projects 3 metres (10 ft) over a sheer cliff. It required considerable nerve to place incense on its head then walk backwards to safety.

Dos and don'ts: There is plenty of steep walking to be done in the Wudang Mountains, and countless steps, so bring sturdy shoes. You can join hiking tours, which last up to three days.

central to Taoism, and this was also applied to a form of martial arts called Wudang Chuan, said to have been created by the hermit Zhang Sanfeng in the 14th century. It is the parent of a number of modern martial-arts disciplines, including t'ai chi and various schools of kung fu. The Wudang Mountains are famous today for martial-arts teaching, and pupils come from all over the world to attend courses, particularly at the former Xuxu Palace – where the courtyards fill with practitioners performing their balletic moves. There are 72 temples, 9 monasteries, 36 nunneries and 9 palaces in the scattered set of buildings now known as the 'Ancient Building Complex'. They were built over a period of

1,000 years in two main phases, starting with the Tang Dynasty (AD 618–907). It is said that Emperor Taizong ordered the construction of the earliest major building, the Five Dragon Temple, after prayers from Wudang appeared to bring an end to a drought.

The focal point is the northernmost complex, rising up to the Golden Hall on the summit of the Sky Pillar Peak – the highest of the range at 1,612 metres (5,288 ft). This temple was prefabricated for the Yongle Emperor in gold-plated brass in Beijing in 1416, and hauled all the way here, an astonishing feat. This is the highpoint of pilgrimage, a physical struggle

performed by young and old alike (a cable car offers an easy alternative). Today, pilgrims and curious visitors come to walk up and down the steep hills between the temples, and to watch the martial-arts demonstrations. Tourism may have arrived in the Wudang Mountains, but their beauty – like the eternal truths of Taoism – remains undiminished.

A monastery village clings to the steep slopes that lead up to the Golden Hall. Between November and March these mountains are often cloaked in snow.

The Zixiao Taoist temple (also known as the Purple Heaven Palace) fittingly provides the setting for martial-arts training and displays to this day. The palace was founded by the Yongle Emperor (Zhu Di, reigned 1401–24), the creator of the Forbidden City in Beijing. He claimed that he was the reincarnation of the Taoist god Xuan Wu (the 'Perfected Warrior'), who is said to have trained at Wudang.

Latitude 29°39'N **Longitude** 91°7'E

Location Lhasa, Tibet, China

Faith Tibetan Buddhism

Built 1645–94

Approximate area 130,000 square metres
(1.4 million sq ft)

Access Daily guided tours

Lhasa CHINA

PAL BHUTAN

INDIA

INDIA

POTALA PALACE

In Lhasa ('Place of the Gods'), the capital of Tibet, China, the most resolute pilgrims make painfully slow progress towards the Potala Palace: three and a half paces forward, raise hands to the heavens, bend, lie flat on the ground in prostration, rise, repeat. And repeat. And repeat. Some of them have been doing this for months, covering huge distances. Around the base of the palace they will encounter another pilgrimage route, called the Kora, travelled by hundreds of people every day as they make their way clockwise around a path punctuated with sacred images. They spin rows of brass prayer wheels as they pass to release prayers that will bring benefit to all beings, and merit for themselves in this life and the next.

The Potala Palace is – along with the Jokhang Temple nearby – the holiest of all places in Tibet. It is the winter palace of the Dalai Lama, the living reincarnation of Avalokiteshvara, the bodhisattva of Compassion. Bodhisattvas are supreme, enlightened beings, who have renounced the opportunity to become a Buddha (and thus enter nirvana) in order to remain bodhisattvas and continue to be reborn, so they can help human beings in need until all have been saved – which is, effectively, for ever.

The current, 14th Dalai Lama has not lived here since 1959: he has resided in India since the age of 23. But the Red Palace part of the complex still contains the revered tombs of eight previous Dalai Lamas stretching back

Fearsome creatures guard an entrance gate to the palace against evil: dogs bare their teeth, and demonic figures scowl from the bosses below. Influenced by the rich and colourful mythology of the native Bon religion, much of popular Tibetan Buddhism centres on the need to appease malevolent deities.

TRAVELLER'S **TIPS**

Best time to go: Despite Lhasa's great altitude, the weather is relatively mild all year. April to October is a good time to travel, with July to September best of all.

Look out for: The jewel-encrusted, seventh-century image of Arya Lokeshvara (or Avalokitesvara), once belonging to Songtsen Gampo.

Dos and don'ts: Lhasa is 3,750 metres (12,300 ft) above sea level; mountain sickness is common – take care to acclimatize.

to the 17th century. Their embalmed bodies are entombed in large, bell-shaped stupas, which are covered in gold and studded with jewels and semi-precious stones.

With its thick, tapering walls rising like a extension of the Marpo Ri ('Red Hill') on which it rests, the Potala Palace is one of the world's most distinctive buildings. The site was said to be a cave used for meditation by the seventh-century King Songtsen Gampo, who is credited with introducing Buddhism to Tibet. He married a Chinese princess, who brought with her the revered Jowo Shakyamuni statue now in the Jokhang Temple, and he built a fort on the Marpo Ri to live in. A thousand years later, in 1645, the fifth Dalai Lama started building the new palace on the site; it took nearly 50 years to complete. It was extended to its present proportions by the 13th Dalai Lama in the early 1900s.

There are two distinct parts to the Potala: the Red Palace (painted deep red on the outside) is reserved for religious functions and contains the stupas of the Dalai Lamas, plus numerous shrines and sacred treasures. This is effectively surrounded by the White Palace, which contains the living quarters of the Dalai Lama and the monks, and was the centre of government and administration for Tibet.

The building rises to 13 storeys in some parts, and there are more than 1,000 rooms. Much of the inside is sumptuously decorated, the walls covered in motifs in vivid colours – carmine red, saturated blue, marigold yellow – and murals depicting stories from the scriptures and images of the Buddha. There are numerous sacred paintings on canvas scrolls, called *tankas*, plus textile hangings, carpets and cushions. Chapels, niches and display cases are filled with precious statues or ornate shrines, decked with jewels.

Today the Potala Palace is designated a museum, and has undergone a 20-year restoration programme. This has not removed entirely the patina of age that comes with centuries of usage. Nor has it removed its intense spirituality – deemed worthy of a journey of 100,000 prostrations.

Prayer flags decorate various points around the palace. They are not there simply for adornment, but to carry prayers as they flutter in the breeze.

MOUNT FUJI

It should be no surprise that Mount Fuji is sacred. It is a mountain of exceptional beauty, drawing the eye from afar, and often visible from Tokyo, 100 kilometres (60 miles) to the northeast. Artists have always been fascinated by it, most famously the great printmaker Hokusai, who created his well-known series *Thirty-Six Views of Mount Fuji* in the 1820s.

Seeing Mount Fuji from all angles reveals that it is a near-symmetrical volcanic cone, shaped by its last eruption in 1707–8. It remains cloaked in snow for much of the year, lending it an air of pristine purity, although it is often coyly shrouded in cloud. Not simply the highest mountain in Japan, rising to 3,776 metres (12,388 ft), it is also the most sacred of its Three Holy Mountains (the others being Mount Tate and Mount Haku). In ancient times it was revered by the original inhabitants of Japan, the Ainu, who would have witnessed it in its more active stage: the word Fuji may derive from their fire god Fuchi. It is sacred to Shinto, Japan's native religion, which sees all natural features – and especially mountains – as dwelling places of the spirits called *kami*. The kami of Mount Fuji is the goddess Sengen-sama, also known as Konohanasakuya-hime, a life-force associated with the blossoming of trees. If due respect is paid to Sengen-sama, she will prevent the volcano from erupting.

The Shiraito Falls, in the southwestern foothills of Mount Fuji, are fed by spring water from the mountain and were held sacred by the Fuji cults. They are in full flow in summer when flushed with winter snow-melt. The Shiraito Falls form part of the Fuji-Hakone-Izu National Park, which consists of a patchwork of dispersed beauty spots and natural wonders, including the Fuji Five Lakes.

JAPAN

Tokyo

Mount Fuji

Latitude 35°21'N **Longitude** 138°43'E

Location East central Honshu island, Japan

Faith Shinto, Buddhist

Age Pilgrimage route: from AD 663

Approximate area 1,800 square kilometres (695 sq miles)

Access Free access all year; the recommended climbing season is July–August

The view of Mount Fuji from Lake Yamanaka shows its near-perfect cone, here reflected in the water. The lake is the largest of the Fuji Five Lakes that form an arc around the mountain's northern flank.

Although the mountain is sacred, it is not taboo to climb Mount Fuji. Indeed, climbing Mount Fuji is a way of doing honour to Sengen-sama, as well as to one of the great national symbols of Japan. Buddhists see it as a metaphor for the path to enlightenment, rising from the earthly verdant base, through the treeline to the higher levels of red, bare volcanic debris – the realm of the gods and death. To make the journey and return is a kind of purification ritual. The Shugendo sect, which emerged after the seventh century AD, embracing a blend of Buddhist and Shinto beliefs, asserted that mountains provide the perfect setting to communicate with the gods and the kami, and integrated mountain climbing with their devotions. Another sect called Fujiko focused uniquely on Mount Fuji, following the teachings of Hasegawa Kakugyo who promoted the concept of the religious ascent of the mountain in the 16th century.

Set paths up the mountain developed over the centuries, and are now punctuated with shrines, teahouses and *torii* gates (these are Shinto monuments that mark the threshold between the profane and sacred). One path starting from the north began with the Kitaguchi Hongu Sengen Jinja (North Entrance Sengen Main Shrine), a beautiful Shinto temple said to date from AD 788, set among ancient trees and dedicated to Sengen-sama. Above it lies the route to the top, which is called the Yoshida Guchi (trail). The Shugendo developed the southern Murayama route, now called the Fujinomiya Guchi.

Most Japanese today hope to make a pilgrimage to the top of Mount Fuji at least once in their lifetime. And some 400,000 do so every year – mainly in the official two-month climbing season in July and August, when the mountain is snow-free. As a result, the popular trails may be packed with people, shuffling along one behind another. The dream is to be at the summit for sunrise, and large accommodation huts – with restaurants and shops and toilet blocks – are found at various waystations, ready to help visitors achieve their goal. Climbing to the top is still a tough proposition, a relentless uphill hike, often in the cold and wind.

After five or more hours, the climbers reach the summit, where there is a *torii* gate and a shrine to Sengen-sama, as well as souvenir shops and snack bars. There is no forced sense of reverence here, but a huge feeling of achievement. Exhausted, the pilgrims head down the mountain to catch the bus home.

The Chureito Peace Pagoda at the Arakura Sengen Shrine in Fujiyoshida, to the west of Tokyo, is a famous place from which to view Mount Fuji, especially when the cherry trees are in blossom in spring.

KINKAKU-JI

Kinkaku means Golden Pavilion, and this beautiful building was the centrepiece of a paradise garden in north Kyoto, created in 1397 by the third Muromachi shogun, Ashikaga Yoshimitsu, for his retirement. Set over the Kyoko-chi ('Mirror Pond'), surrounded by landscaped gardens that change mood with every season, it is a pavilion of extraordinary poise and elegance. The upper storeys are sheathed in gold leaf, hence the name. The whole ensemble was an interpretation of a *jodo-teien*: a garden modelled on a classic description of an imagined Buddhist paradise, which should contain a pond, lotus flowers, and – subtly integrated with the landscape – a hall decorated with gold, silver and precious stones.

The tiered, curving roofs of the Golden Pavilion shelter a delicate wooden structure surrounded by verandas, which provide a bridge between the natural scene outside and the interior architecture. The ground floor has removable screens, giving open views onto the pond.

Each of the floors has been designed in a different style. The ground floor, in contrasting natural, unpainted wood, is in a Japanese domestic style developed for spaces in palaces to be used for performances of Noh drama and dance. The middle floor, in samurai style, was used for composing poetry. The upper floor, in Chinese style, was for meditation. A gilded phoenix crests the roof, a Japanese symbol of fire, the sun, justice and loyalty.

After Ashikaga Yoshimitsu died in 1408, the property was bequeathed to the Kyoto-based Shokoku-ji branch of the Rinzai school of Zen Buddhism and it became a temple complex, acquiring the suffix -ji: although formally called the Rokuon-ji (Deer Garden Temple), it became popularly known as Kinkaku-ji. Architecturally, this was not a problem, since Zen temple architecture was very similar to lay architecture. In any case, the Golden Temple was not intended as a place of worship: it is, rather, a *shari-den*, a storehouse of sacred relics and statues. When the screens on the ground floor are pushed back, they reveal statues of the Buddha alongside Ashikaga Yoshimitsu.

The Golden Temple, therefore, is only a part of an extensive complex, which includes the Kuri (living quarters for monks and priests), and the Hojo (the abbot's house). It also has a

The Golden Temple was not seen as a place of worship. It was designed to be viewed from a distance in its landscape setting.

Latitude 35°2'N Longitude 135°43'E
Location Kyoto, central Japan
Faith Zen Buddhism
Built Originally 1397
Approximate area 4 hectares (10 acres)
Access Ticketed entry; open daily

JAPAN

Kinkaku-ji

Osaka

classic teahouse, the Sekkatei, designed with studied modesty and simplicity by the tea master Kanamori Sowa in the early 17th century.

Progression along pathways and bridges around the gardens is designed to lead visitors to the various sites and shrines and to reveal changing views upon which to meditate. The Kyoko-chi pond is dotted with small islands, many with stories attached, replete with symbolism: a line of stones is seen as a group of sailing boats heading for the Island of Eternal Life. The waterfall called Ryumon-baku, between the Kyoko-chi pond and the Anmin-taku pond, recalls the Toryumon legend of carp (represented here by the large rock beneath the falling water): it said that if they could climb a waterfall, they would become (good) dragons – suggesting that anyone can achieve ambitions by endeavour. A monument on an island in the Anmin-taku pond is called White Snake Mound, dedicated to the serpent that serves as a messenger to the gods – although another tale says that White Snake was the name of one of Ashikaga Yoshimitsu's many mistresses, who drowned herself in the pond in a fit of jealousy.

The gardens are believed to be much as Ashikaga Yoshimitsu would have seen them, and he may well have known some of the oldest pines. However, much of the original temple complex – except the Golden Pavilion – was destroyed in the Onin War of 1467–77. The Golden Pavilion survived until 1950, when it was burned down by a deranged young monk. What we see today is a faithful reconstruction, completed in 1955. It has lost none of its mesmeric beauty. The world is in a constant state of flux, and nothing is quite what it seems – as Zen Buddhism constantly reminds us.

Statues of the Buddhist divinity Jizo at Kinkaku-ji. Jizo, usually depicted as a monk, is seen as the guardian of children, particularly those who have died before their parents or babies that have been miscarried or stillborn; the name can be translated as 'Earth Treasury' or 'Earth Womb'. Here thousands of one-yen coins have been thrown around the statues, perhaps by parents wishing for protection for their lost children.

Rocks were selected and positioned in the pond to create satisfying views upon which to meditate. Some can be interpreted as symbols of the seas and mountains.

ANGKOR WAT

The view across the moat is a picture of the Hindu Universe, with Mount Meru rising out of the oceans – today embellished with the pompom heads of towering sugar-palm trees.

So significant and iconic is Angkor Wat to the Cambodian people that their national flag features a silhouetted outline of the place. It is the largest spiritual complex on Earth, and a place regularly proposed as the eighth wonder of the world.

Angkor Wat is also the best-preserved architectural site of the Khmer Empire (AD 802–1431). In its heyday, the Khmer Empire controlled most of mainland Southeast Asia, covering not just modern Cambodia, but most of Thailand and Laos. Its capital, Angkor (meaning 'City'), set just to the north of the 'Great Lake' of Tonlé Sap, was one of the largest cities in the world, with a population of perhaps 750,000.

TRAVELLER'S TIPS

Best time to go: November to February is relatively dry and cool, and the most popular season. March to May are the hottest months, and June to October is the rainy season.

Look out for: The five towers of Angkor Wat appear on the flag of Cambodia, a measure of the temple's status as a symbol of the nation.

Dos and don'ts: Do visit some of the scores of outlying temples. Many are as intricate as Angkor Wat, but less visited, and some remain eerily clasped by the roots of strangler-fig trees.

This was a Hindu country, having had contact with India for nearly 1,000 years. The Khmer god-kings built a series of magnificent temples at Angkor, starting from around AD 880. The greatest and most famous of all is the stunning Angkor Wat, which was built during the reign of King Suryavarman II (1113–50). It was meticulously designed as an image of the universe, within concentric squares (a symbolic map of the earth), laid out to the points of the compass. At the centre are five towers, carved in the shape of lotus buds, representing the five peaks of Mount Meru, the mythical home of the Hindu gods. The temple as a whole was dedicated to Vishnu. Lining the walls of an inner courtyard, in long strips of stone panels, are detailed, intricate bas relief sculptures, recounting tales from the Hindu holy books, the Mahabharata and the Ramayana, and the stories of Khmer conquests.

All around Angkor Wat is a square moat, now dappled with waterlilies, representing the oceans. Water was a central feature of the city, which included a network of canals and two colossal, rectangular reservoirs, the East Baray and the West Baray, holding water within raised dykes. These were key components in a sophisticated rice-growing culture, which, by irrigation, could produce food through the wet and the dry seasons, and raise two or three crops a year.

THAILAND   LAOS

Angkor Wat
• Siem Reap
CAMBODIA

VIETNAM

Latitude 13°24'N **Longitude** 103°52'E

Location Siem Reap Province, northern Cambodia

Faith Hindu and Buddhist

Built 1113–50

Approximate area 93 hectares (230 acres)

Access 1, 3 and 7-day passes, purchased at the site

91

The city itself ran 24 kilometres (15 miles) from east to west and 8 kilometres (5 miles) from north to south. Scattered across this area are 72 major temples and other monuments; they survived because they are made of stone and brick.

In 1177 Angkor was invaded by the Champa people of Vietnam. When it recovered under King Jayavarman VII, it turned to Buddhism, and his Bayon temple at the heart of the extensive Angkor Thom ('Great City') – built on another square ground-plan just to the north of Angkor Wat – has numerous towers bearing faces of the Buddha, or bodhisattvas (enlightened beings), turned to the four compass points.

In around 1430 the Khmer Empire collapsed and most of Angkor was abandoned to the encroaching jungle – although Angkor Wat itself remained largely clear as a Buddhist monastery ('Wat'). It came to international attention after 1860 and during French colonial rule, and a massive archaeological programme ran for decades until it was abandoned in the face of civil war in 1972. A fresh round of restoration has been going on since the 1990s, assisted by income from the 500,000 people who now come to visit Angkor Wat every year, in search of some ineluctable connection with a lost and irretrievable past.

The 12th-century temple of Ta Prohm is gripped by the roots of huge silk-cotton and strangler-fig trees, creating one of the most evocative and other-worldly images of the Angkor Wat complex: a precious ancient ruin overtaken by the jungle. These invasive trees present a constant worry for conservationists: as they grow they push the stone apart, and when they eventually topple they take the stone with them.

The approach to the south gate of Angkor Thom is lined with 54 statues on either side, including benevolent guardian *devas*, who feature in both Hindu and Buddhist mythology.

Latitude 24°41'N **Longitude** 84°59'E	
Location Bihar, northeast India	
Faith Buddhist	
Built From about 250 BC	
Approximate area 4.8 hectares (12 acres)	
Access Free access, daily, throughout the year	

The main monument, next to the Bodhi Tree, is an elaborately carved tower of brick and stone, originally built about 1,500 years ago. An inner chamber contains a golden statue of the Buddha.

MAHABODHI TEMPLE

The extensive compound about the Mahabodhi Temple contains thousands of devotional mementoes left by pilgrims, including festoons of prayer flags, often inscribed with prayers. They mirror the global appeal of Bodh Gaya: pilgrims come here from all over the world, representing the many branches of Buddhism, each of which has temples, monasteries and lodgings in the city.

Renouncing wealth, high status and his young family, Prince Siddhartha Gautama spent several years on a spiritual quest to solve the suffering of the world before, in about 530 BC, he sat beneath a banyan tree by the River Falgu and – quite suddenly – became the Buddha, the 'Enlightened One'. He spent the next seven weeks meditating around this 'Bodhi tree' (tree of enlightenment), before setting off on his travels around India and Nepal to spread his message, until his death in Kushinagar some 40 years later at the age of 80.

The scene of his enlightenment became the most treasured pilgrimage destination in Buddhism. In about 250 BC the great Buddhist emperor Ashoka built the first Mahabodhi Temple next to the Bodhi Tree. A town grew up around it, eventually taking its current name Bodh Gaya. It flourished for more than a thousand years, until the arrival of Islam in India and the rule of the Delhi Sultanate in the 13th century. The Mahabodhi Temple fell victim to neglect; the Bodhi Tree died. Then in the late 19th century, under British rule, and at the instigation of Burmese Buddhists, it was restored, and a new Bodhi Tree was planted – said to be a sapling propagated from the Sri Mahabodhi Tree in Sri Lanka, itself a cutting from the original tree, taken there by the daughter of Ashoka.

Within the temple compound there are shrines that commemorate the activity of the Buddha during each of those seven weeks. Parts of the park are crammed with stupas and stone inscriptions tracing a history of 2,500 years of devotion. But the main focus is the sacred Bodhi Tree, beneath which Buddhism began.

TRAVELLER'S TIPS

Best time to go: For the most agreeable weather, go in winter: October to March. December is a high point: it is the traditional visiting time of the Tibetans and the Dalai Lama.

Look out for: The Great Buddha statue in Bodh Gaya: 25 metres (82 ft) high, built in red granite and sandstone, the collective work of 120,000 masons; it was consecrated by the Dalai Lama in 1989.

Dos and don'ts: Travel to or from Bodh Gaya in the day – there may be armed bandits on the road at night.

VARANASI

Latitude 25°16'N **Longitude** 82°57'E	
Location Uttar Pradesh, northeast India	
Faith Primarily Hindu	
Age c.3,000 years	
Approximate area 1,550 square kilometres (600 sq miles)	
Access Free access, although some temples are off-limits	

As the River Ganges journeys eastwards across northern India towards the ocean it turns briefly to the north near Varanasi (called Benares in former times). The city clusters along the west bank. At dawn, the soft, golden light of the rising sun spills across the open plain opposite and catches first the crest of spires and towers – the *sikharas* ('mountain peaks') – of the

temples, before progressing down the long steps of the *ghats* to the river's edge. This is the moment that tens of thousands of Hindus – local residents as well as pilgrims from afar – have been waiting for: the moment when the eternal sun kisses the sacred waters of the Mother Ganges. Bathing in the water, drinking it, holding it up to the sun in cupped hands while performing the prayers of *puja* – all bring blessings and the forgiveness of sins. Although in reality heavily polluted, the water of the Ganges is held to be spiritually pure, and has the power to grant *moksha*: final liberation from the interminable cycle of life and death and rebirth.

There is a serenity here, but this is not a place of forced reverence. Pilgrims wash and splash and chatter, children dart about, laundry workers whack wet clothes against boards. Hundreds of large rowing boats filled with sightseers – from India and abroad – hover offshore to view the scene. The 7 kilometres (4 miles) of water frontage is a ramshackle mix of stepped ghats, shabby concrete buildings tiered with balconies, ashrams and temples, umbrellas, signage, power lines, mud banks and heaped rubbish.

And among all this are the funeral pyres on the Shamshan ghats, burning day and night. Bodies wrapped in cloth are

The ghats have an ethereal calm early in the morning, before the hordes of visitors and pilgrims arrive.

carried on bamboo stretchers through the narrow alleys behind
the ghats to be burned on wood fires at the water's edge. Then
the ashes are thrown into the river. To have this privilege is to
be given the best chance of achieving *moksha*.

For the most part, there is little ceremony attached
to these cremations: it is a transaction. At Varanasi,
death is mundane. There may even be bodies
floating in the river, often those of old sadhus –
the itinerant, freewheeling monks who
abandon the material world in the
quest for spiritual liberation, living

TRAVELLER'S TIPS

Best time to go: October to March to avoid the great heat of April–May and the
monsoon season (June–September). It can be cold at night in December and January.

Look out for: The much-respected Banaras Hindu University (the 'Oxford of the East')
has a good museum of art and archaeology called the Bharat Kala Bhavan.

Dos and don'ts: Do not take photos of cremation pyres; best to keep your camera out
of sight. Also, for security reasons, do not take photos in the neighbourhood of the
Gyanvapi Mosque.

outside society yet within it. The Aghori sadhus challenge the taboos of death by smearing themselves with cremation ash and drinking from skulls.

The Aghori sadhus are devotees of Shiva, the creator and destroyer, one of the most powerful in the vast and complex pantheon of Hindu gods, and often placed alongside Vishnu and Brahma to form a trinity. Varanasi, one of India's most sacred cities, is above all the city of Shiva. The Ganges is said to flow through Shiva's long hair, which prevented it from flooding when the goddess Ganga, daughter of Himavat, god of snow, poured water upon the earth from heaven. At Varanasi, Shiva rose up through the earth's crust in a fiery pillar of light to soar to the heavens, leaving his symbol, the phallic lingam, to mark the spot. This Jyotirlingam, the ultimate focus of pilgrimage to Varanasi, is the centrepiece of the city's most holy temple, the Vishwanath Temple – otherwise known as the Golden Temple for the ton of gold that covers its spires and dome.

Chaotic yet serene, tumbledown and bejewelled, drab but flared with vivid colour, money-grabbing and ethereally pious, a city of timeless tradition fretful with modern pressures, Varanasi is as varied, contradictory and compelling as the Hindu pantheon to which it is so intimately bound.

Worshippers come to the river's edge at sunrise to bathe and wash and offer prayers – each with their own interpretation of the power and significance of the holy river. For many pilgrims this is a once-in-a-lifetime experience, for locals it is a daily duty. 'Fortunate are the people who reside on the banks of the Ganga,' says an inscription on the wall of a ghat.

Scores of boats carry pilgrims and worshippers away from the crowds on the ghats so they can have time to themselves on the sacred river.

प्रयाग घाट
PRAYAG GHAT

THE GOLDEN TEMPLE OF AMRITSAR

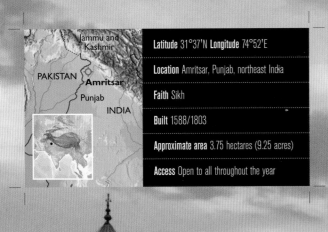

Latitude 31°37'N **Longitude** 74°52'E	
Location Amritsar, Punjab, northeast India	
Faith Sikh	
Built 1588/1803	
Approximate area 3.75 hectares (9.25 acres)	
Access Open to all throughout the year	

Beneath a radiant blue sky, afloat on its stone island in the middle of a huge blue-green lake, the Golden Temple glints and dazzles in the sharp Indian sun. All around, pristine white buildings line the marbled walkways on the square rim of the lake, forming a protective cordon to the precious shrine, while keeping a respectful distance. This is one of the world's most beautiful sacred places: its beauty alone brings exclamations of awe from visitors. There is a deep sense of sanctity here, and, more surprisingly, tranquillity – surprisingly because the Golden Temple is visited by some 80,000 people every day, and sometimes 200,000.

They come mainly because this is the most sacred site of the Sikh religion. This is where the fourth Sikh guru (or leader), Guru Ram Das, settled in about 1574, next to the sacred pool called Amritsar, 'the lake of the nectar of immortality', long cherished by holy men and mystics. In 1588 the fifth guru, Guru Arjan Dev, began work on the first Gurdwara (Sikh temple) on the lake. This was destroyed by invaders from

TRAVELLER'S **TIPS**

Best time to go: Autumn (October and November) for the best climate. Summer is extremely hot, and winter is chilly (cooled by the Himalayas). Weekends are busier than weekdays.

Look out for: The temple's Guru Ka Langar is the world's largest community kitchen, feeding some 40,000 people every day. You are welcome to lend a hand.

Dos and don'ts: Pilgrims and visitors alike have to remove their shoes on entering the temple and wash their feet, and to cover their heads (scarves are provided).

Afghanistan in 1761, but in 1803 the powerful Sikh ruler Maharaja Ranjit Singh replaced it with the temple we see today. It is formally known as the Hari Mandir Sahib ('Temple of God'), but in the 1830s the upper storeys were sheathed in gold, lending it the name by which the world now knows it.

Following the decree of the 10th guru, Gobind Singh, in 1699, the 11th and permanent guru was, and remains, the holy book of Sikhism, the Adi Granth – or Sri Guru Granth Sahib, as it now became known. It is this holy book that is the focus of all attention at the Golden Temple. Every day at dawn, thousands of pilgrims join a procession to bring a

venerated copy from its overnight resting place in the Akal Takht temple and across the long footbridge leading from the shore to the Golden Temple. All day, sacred texts are read and chanted from the book as pilgrims queue to pass through the temple and pay their respects. The visitors stop, offer gifts, pray, contemplate, then move on to allow others to follow.

At night, the Sri Guru Granth Sahib is ceremoniously paraded back to the shore, again accompanied by thousands, chanting to trumpets and drums and throwing rose petals – against the backdrop of the Golden Temple and the peripheral towers and domes spellbindingly illuminated beneath the night sky.

Viewed from across the 'lake of the nectar of immortality', the Golden Temple has a regal quality, vividly contrasting with the white buildings that stand around it like respectful courtiers.

Sikhs make up the vast majority of the visitors, of course. But in the spirit of Sikhism – which promotes equality for all, regardless of race, gender or religion – everyone is welcome. All, too, are invited to participate in a free, simple meal of chapatis and lentil dhal, prepared daily by an army of volunteers. Anyone may also stay the night for free in one of the dormitories.

All these facilities – as well as libraries, shrines to saints and martyrs, the Sikh parliament at the Akal Takht, meeting rooms, first-aid posts and offices – are located in the buildings set around the lake and the adjacent complex. This includes the Central Sikh Museum, which bears witness to some of the historic strife that has shaped the religion, and the proud warrior traditions that have underpinned it. As recently as 1984, conflict with the Indian government led to a much-resented invasion of the Golden Temple complex by security forces, resulting in considerable damage.

For many Sikhs, visiting the Golden Temple is a lifetime's ambition, and they come with their families from right around the globe, often to mark a special occasion in their lives. Others come regularly, perhaps every year, to relive anew the profound sense of peace and reconciliation that they experience here, uplifted by the sheer beauty of the place and the positive, reaffirming values that participation in its rituals imparts.

The Darshani Deorhi (entrance gate) is a large pavilion-like building that serves as the gateway at the shore end of the causeway. Its central archway is adorned with gold panels, elaborately sculpted and embossed with images and texts from the holy scriptures. It serves as a fitting and tantalizing introduction to the Golden Temple.

Devotees sit and reflect in front of the illuminated Golden Temple, paying their respects to the holy book – the Sri Guru Granth Sahib.

TAJ MAHAL

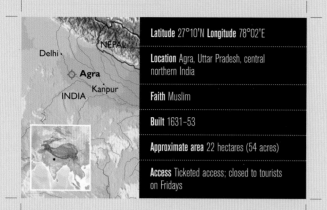

Latitude 27°10'N **Longitude** 78°02'E	
Location Agra, Uttar Pradesh, central northern India	
Faith Muslim	
Built 1631–53	
Approximate area 22 hectares (54 acres)	
Access Ticketed access; closed to tourists on Fridays	

Perfect, sublime, afloat between earth and heaven – few dissent from the superlatives that are applied to the Taj Mahal. Even though countless photographs have made it so familiar, its profoundly satisfying proportions, immaculate whiteness and finesse in detail still bring tears to the eyes of many of the two million or so people who come to see it every year from all over the world.

Tears, too, because this is a monument to human, romantic love, and the inevitability of its demise and separation in death. The Taj Mahal was built by Shah Jehan, 'King of the World', one of the richest and most successful of the Mughal emperors, who had united most of India and the subcontinent for the first time in nearly 2,000 years. Agra was his capital, where he lived surrounded by luxury at his palace in the Red Fort. He had a harem and three wives, but his favourite was Arjumand Banu, whom he called Mumtaz Mahal, 'Chosen One of the Palace'. Similar in age, they had been betrothed as young teenagers, and married in 1612, when Mumtaz Mahal was 19. Their love and affection for each other – unusual at court at the time – was remarked upon by chroniclers: 'The intimacy, deep affection, attention and favour which his majesty had for Mumtaz Mahal exceeded a thousand times what he felt for any other.'

When she died in 1631, giving birth to their 14th child, Shah Jehan was inconsolable. His response was to build her the most beautiful of all Mughal mausoleums, the Taj Mahal, 'Crown of the Palaces', on a bend of the River Yamuna in Agra, within sight of the Red Fort.

With its immaculate symmetry reflected in the central channel, representing one of the four rivers of paradise, the Taj Mahal is one of the world's most beautifully proportioned buildings.

TRAVELLER'S TIPS

Best time to go: October, November and February, to avoid great heat and monsoons. Go at 6 a.m. to beat the crowds, and again later to see the complex in a different light (tickets are valid for a day).

Look out for: Optical illusions: the Taj Mahal seems to get smaller as you walk through the arch of the Great Gate. Also, to make them appear vertical, the minarets lean slightly outwards.

Dos and don'ts: Do check whether your visit coincides with a full moon. Tickets for night-viewing give access to the southern end of the complex; take mosquito repellent.

Were it not the prelude to the Taj Mahal, the Great Gate would be considered a masterpiece. Its red sandstone is a deliberate contrast to prevent it from challenging the main event.

For the project, Shah Jehan brought together all the resources of his empire and its trading partners, with no expense spared: his greatest architects and craftsmen, the finest white marble from Rajasthan, and precious and semi-precious stones from India, Ceylon, Afghanistan, Tibet and Arabia to fill the delicate inlay decorations.

But the Taj Mahal is more than an exquisite building. It is a re-creation of the Muslim paradise, with the tomb of Mumtaz Mahal its heart. The word 'paradise' is derived from the Persian for walled garden, and this is how the heavenly paradise is described in the Koran and Islamic texts. In front of the magnificent domes and minarets of the Taj Mahal lie the gardens, divided by four intersecting canals: the four rivers of paradise, meeting at a raised marble tank representing the holy mountain from which the rivers flow. The sacred number four is repeated in the four gardens, each divided into four, laid to lawn since the days of the British Raj, but formerly filled with roses, daffodils and blossoming fruit trees.

The whole of the Taj Mahal complex was conceived as a progression from earth to heaven. At the southern end of the rectangular, walled complex is an earthly bazaar or market, laid out to the same ground-plan as the gardens. The Taj Mahal is accessed from the south through the monumental Great Gate in contrasting red sandstone, emerging to views up the gardens to the mausoleum, which is reflected in the central water course. A mosque, also in red sandstone, flanks the mausoleum to the west, balanced to the east by a twin building – symmetry being an essential expression of perfection in Islamic architecture.

Within the octagonal Taj Mahal, eight chambers surround the airy, ornately decorated central chamber that houses Mumtaz Mahal's cenotaph – eight for the eight levels of the Muslim heaven. The larger cenotaph beside hers is that of Shah Jehan himself, providing the only element of asymmetry in the entire complex. Their bodies are in fact not here, but in similarly simple, but delicately inlaid tombs in a much plainer room below, conforming to the Islamic requirement of simplicity in graves.

Shortly after the Taj Mahal was completed in 1653, Shah Jehan was deposed by Aurangzeb, a son of Mumtaz Mahal, who – as was the tradition – promptly slaughtered his rival brothers. He imprisoned his father in the Red Fort, where he died, a broken man, in 1666, aged 74. There is a myth that Shah Jehan had intended to build a mirror image of the Taj Mahal, but in black marble, as his own mausoleum, in gardens on the other side of the River Yamuna. But he was surely content to be laid to rest in his greatest creation, the world's most beautiful building, next to the great love of his life.

ULURU

Alice Springs·
◇ **Uluru**
AUSTRALIA

Latitude 25°20'S **Longitude** 131°02'E	
Location Northern Territory, central Australia	
Faith Tjukurpa (Dreamtime)	
Age More than 10,000 years	
Approximate area 3.3 square kilometres (1.3 sq miles)	
Access Ticketed entry (3-day pass) to the park	

A bold, rust-red in its natural state, Uluru subtly changes colour according to the weather and the daily progression of the sun, lending it character, moods and unfathomable mystery.

'This rock appears more wonderful every time I look at it,' wrote the Australian explorer William Gosse in 1873, choosing to name it after the Premier of South Australia, Sir Henry Ayers. Everyone has the same reaction to this astonishing, isolated landmass that surges bizarrely out of the dusty red plain at the very heart of Australia. The local Aboriginal people, the Anangu, have thought so for some 10,000 years. Their name, Uluru, has now been restored to it, and since 2002 has been given lead billing in the official title Uluru/Ayers Rock.

Uluru is a single clump of sedimentary rock called arkose – crystalline, feldspar-rich sandstone. Thrown up by a mountain-building episode in the earth's crust 530 million years ago, it has resisted the erosion which flattened all that had once enclosed it.

The Anangu, like all Aboriginal people, attach great spiritual importance to natural landmarks. In their eyes, these were laid down by eternal Creator Beings – animals, plants and humans – as they progressed across the continent, and continue to do so in an ongoing story of creation called Dreamtime (Tjukurpa to the Anangu). The paths and associated customs that link the landmarks are called songlines.

Naturally, a landmark as astonishing as Uluru, at the meeting point of many songlines, makes it a potent spiritual place, where gatherings, rituals and initiation ceremonies take place. The Anangu will not walk on Uluru, such is their respect for it, but rather progress around it. Caves and crevices have been decorated in rock paintings. Every feature recalls one of many Tjukurpa stories, about Mala the reddish-brown hare-wallaby, Liru the poisonous snake and Kuniya the woman python.

Despite being a bare and parched rock in the arid Red Centre of Australia, Uluru is surrounded by a rim of surprisingly fertile land. Eucalyptus trees and low-lying shrubs such as desert figs benefit from the water run-off from the rock after rare and fickle – but sometimes heavy – rains, which collects in pools and waterholes, and traditionally provides a rich source of sustenance for Aboriginal gatherings.

TRAVELLER'S TIPS

Best time to go: Sunrise and sunset. In spring (September–November), wild flowers carpet the dunes. Winter (June–August) has pleasant daytime temperatures, but nights can be cold.

Look out for: The Uluru-Kata Tjuta Cultural Centre offers a full introduction to Anangu life and beliefs, including Tjukurpa, song, dance and ceremonies, arts and crafts and bush tucker food.

Dos and don'ts Climbing Uluru is not prohibited, except in high winds. Don't do it, however, if you wish to respect the beliefs of the Anangu people. Instead walk the 9.4-kilometre (5.8-mile) trail around the base.

Coated in gold leaf and crowned by a golden, spire-like stupa, the Golden Rock glitters all day, as the sun – a corresponding orb – makes its tour around and over its prominent location.

GOLDEN ROCK

Latitude 17°29'N **Longitude** 97°5'E	
Location Mon State, southern Burma (Myanmar)	
Faith Buddhist	
Built c.16th century	
Approximate area 50 square metres (540 sq ft)	
Access Ticketed, all day and night throughout the year	

The Golden Rock's alleged direct connection with the Buddha inspires the devotion of monks from all over Burma and beyond. It is the third most important pilgrimage site in Burma after the Shwedagon Pagoda in Yangon (Rangoon), which contains Buddha relics, and the Mahamuni Pagoda near Mandalay, home to a golden image of the Buddha said to have been made in his lifetime.

This huge granite boulder, precariously perched on a cliff edge, looks as though it should roll off its base with the slightest nudge. But it is said to be held in place by a single hair from the head of the Buddha. Legend tells us that a hermit was given the hair by the Buddha himself. He kept it in his own topknot for safe keeping, and when near death, gave it to his king, asking him to create a pagoda for it in the shape of his head. The king called upon the god Thagyamin to help him, and he located a suitable boulder at the bottom of the ocean; it was brought to the top of the mountain in a barge, which was then itself turned to stone. The Burmese name for the Golden Rock is Kyaikhtiyo, which means 'pagoda carried on the hermit's head'.

This is one of the three most sacred Buddhist sites in Burma (also known as Myanmar). For some 500 years pilgrims have come to offer their devotions to the rock, walking up a 11-kilometre (7-mile) track from the nearby town of Kinpun, or – more recently – taking a car or truck up to a point 2.5 kilometres (1.5 miles) beneath the summit. Paved paths and steps lead to the top, but it is still a tough climb, especially in bare feet, as is the tradition.

Today the summit is a busy modern temple complex, with shrines to various Burmese gods and spirits called *nats*, as well as shops, restaurants and a guesthouse. The Golden Rock is surrounded by viewing platforms, used mainly by women. An iron footbridge crosses a chasm to link the temple complex to the small natural plinth on which the Golden Rock stands, rimmed with gilded lotus leaves. Only men come here, for only men are permitted to touch the rock. Many of them bring gold leaf to fix to the rock. This is what makes it sparkle so brilliantly – especially at sunrise and sunset. And on New Year's Eve and on the night of the full moon in the lunar month of Thadingyut, it glitters in the light of 9,000 candles set around its base.

Latitude 8°20'S **Longitude** 115°30'E	
Location Eastern Bali, Indonesia	
Faith Hindu	
Built Besakih temple: from c.1000 AD	
Approximate area 225 square kilometres (86 sq miles)	
Access Free access to the mountain. Besakih: open daily, donations obligatory	

MOUNT AGUNG

Instead of north, east, south and west, the Balinese traditionally orientate themselves along the axis of *kaja* and *kelod*: *kaja* is towards the mountains, and *kelod* is towards the sea. The mountains are the font of blessings: they are the abode of the gods, the source of water to irrigate the rice terraces. The sea is associated with evil, where malign gods lurk, ready to bring harm. The Balinese will always sleep with their heads pointing in the *kaja* direction, given the choice. Temples tend to be aligned along the *kaja* axis, with the most sacred parts nearest to the mountains. And the most sacred of the mountains is Mount Agung ('Great Mountain'), the highest point of this small island, an active volcano, with its peak – often shrouded in cloud – rising to 3,142 metres (10,308 ft).

Bali is a predominantly a Hindu island, a rare exception among the 13,000 or so mainly Muslim islands that make up Indonesia. Hinduism reached Indonesia through trade with India in the second century AD, and became firmly established in the rule of successive Javanese kingdoms. But the arrival of Islam in the 13th century led to a growing power struggle with the Hindu Majapahit Empire in Java; the royal court finally fled to Bali in 1515, where Hinduism was preserved in jealously controlled isolation until the 20th century.

Few places on earth are as closely bonded to their religion as Bali. There are some 20,000 temples here. Little offerings to the gods – called *bali* – are presented daily to the gods and spirits, at shrines, statues, gates, trees, road-crossings, offices, on taxi-drivers' dashboards. Religion is the prime motivation for Bali's rich and intensely skilled culture: gamelan music, dance, theatre – performed for the gods at the countless temple ceremonies that take place every day across the island.

The most sacred of all the temples is Besakih, the 'Mother Temple', perched high on the slopes of Mount Agung. This is a huge complex, embracing 18 individual temple compounds. These are essentially outdoor stage sets awaiting their full purpose at the temple ceremonies, when the gods are deemed to be present. They comprise numerous buildings and monuments, including the many-tiered *meru* towers that represent the mythic Hindu Mahameru, the mountain of the gods – of which, according to local legend, Mount Agung is a fragment.

Thatched with black sugar-palm fibre, they have a faintly intimidating air – and indeed Besakih is noted for its doom-laden atmosphere. Here the darker side of Balinese Hinduism seems palpable – the threat that has to be propitiated by prayer and offerings to keep at bay the kind of world represented by Rangda, the chilling witch who

This view of Mount Agung, from the small island of Nusa Lembongan to the southeast, vividly demonstrates its majestic and imposing scale, as well as the ragged profile of its crater shattered by the 1963 eruption.

appears in the good-versus-evil Barong dance. And not without cause. Seen from afar, Mount Agung rises majestically above emerald rice terraces, frangipani trees and palms. But close-up at Besakih, it has a raw and brooding face. In 1963, after 300 years of dormancy, it showed its power.

Every 100 years Besakih hosts massive purification ceremony called Eka Dasa Rudra. It was supposed to take place in March 1963, but many priests wanted to postpone it, disputing the calculation of the correct date computed from the highly complex Balinese calendars. Clearly the gods were angry – in February that year, Mount Agung began rumbling and emitting puffs of ash and dribbles of lava.

The Indonesian authorities insisted on pushing ahead with the ceremony, as an international conference of tourist agencies was due to attend, along with President Sukarno. It duly took place on 8 March against a backdrop of Mount Agung's growing rage. On 17 March Mount Agung exploded, killing perhaps 2,000 people, and rendering some 100,000 homeless – although Besakih itself was miraculously spared.

It was the ultimate expression of the divine forces that the Balinese, in their daily attendance to their gods, feel they must constantly placate.

TRAVELLER'S **TIPS**

Best time to go: Bali is at its best in the dry season (April–October). January–February can be very wet.

Look out for: Treks lead to the crater of Mount Agung from various points. They usually leave at night, to catch the sunrise. These are tough walks, and you are strongly advised to hire a local guide.

Dos and don'ts: The temperature can be decidedly cool at higher altitudes: take an extra layer of clothing. And try not to lose your cool at Besakih, where tourists are

As Hinduism acknowledges in Shiva and his violent consort Kali, out of destruction comes fertility and rebirth. So it is also with the land: Bali's volcanic soil provides immensely productive farmland, notably in its rice terraces to the south and east of Mount Agung.

A cluster of pagoda-like *meru* towers – always with an odd number of roofs – break the skyline above the temple compounds of Besakih, Bali's 'Mother Temple'. It was probably a place of worship, honouring the holy mountain, before the arrival of Hinduism. But, according to tradition, it was founded in the eighth century AD by a Hindu missionary priest, Danghyang Markandeya, who used it as a place of meditation.

INDONESIA

Semarang
Java
Borobudur Bali

Latitude 7°36'S **Longitude** 110°12'E

Location Central Java, Indonesia

Faith Buddhist

Built C.AD 800

Approximate area 14,400 square metres
(155,500 sq ft)

Access Ticketed guided tours only, daily;
open all year

BOROBUDUR

The setting alone will fill any visitor with wonder. Surrounded by lush greenery, receding into smoky layers of mist at dawn or dusk, Borobudur is framed by jagged, restive peaks of volcanoes. But this artificial stone mountain, prickly with statuary and ornamentation, is far more than a thing of beauty: it is a journey for the soul, laying before pilgrims a virtual Buddhist path from our messy world to the heavenly liberation of nirvana. No one knows for sure when this extraordinarily ambitious project – the largest stone monument in the Southern Hemisphere – was created, but it was probably about 1,200 years ago.

Overlooked by seated Buddhas, first in niches, then in their bell-shaped stupas, the pilgrim passes through 3 kilometres (2 miles) of passageways and staircases lined with sculpted stone panels depicting, in sharp and fluent detail, scenes from each of the parts of this great spiritual journey. First at the lower, square level (symbolic of the earth) we are in our own here-and-now, the world of desire, the Kamadhatu, surrounded by distractions. In the next five, receding square layers we move up into Rupadhatu, the world of forms, to reach the first stages of enlightenment. Then in the three upper, concentric circular layers (symbolic of heaven) we progress to Arupadhatu, the world of formlessness, which fully enlightened Buddhas attain. Here statues of Buddhas, each with their specific posture and hand gesture (*mudra*), look out through the lattice apertures of the stupas to the hills beyond. Lastly we reach the main stupa, which crowns the summit. Beneath are two empty chambers (the only interior spaces to speak of in the whole monument). Did they once contain Buddha statues or sacred relics that have been looted, or did

There are 2,670 bas relief panels at Borobudur, encircling the monument, covering a total distance of some 3 kilometres (2 miles). Some are decorative, but there are also 11 series of narrative panels, telling stories and teaching the lessons of life and the deities. In amongst them are images of village life, temples, weaponry, court, flora and fauna – providing a remarkable record of the times in which Borobudur was built.

The round, heavenly realm sits upon the square earth in this giant cosmological mountain. Little is known about Borobudur's construction, but it must have taken thousands of labourers and stone masons several decades to build.

The top level is encircled by 72 Buddha statues encased in their individual perforated stupas. Only where the stupas are broken are we able to see them clearly.

this signal the glorious void of nirvana, and the final release from *samsara* – the interminable cycle of life and death that blights the existence of those who never achieve Buddhahood? Whatever the case, seen from above, Borobudur looks like a mandala representing the entire Buddhist cosmos.

The history of Borobudur is far from clear. It appears to have been built in around AD 800, during a period when there was friendly rivalry and cooperation between Buddhist and Hindu dynasties in Java. At about the same time the colossal Hindu temple of Prambanan was built just 50 kilometres (31 miles) to the southeast. At some point, however, Borobudur was abandoned, and over time it became coated in volcanic ash and then vegetation, and shaken by earthquakes.

The man who revived interest in Borobudur was Sir Thomas Stamford Raffles, the founder of Singapore, who had been appointed governor of Java after British victory in the Anglo-Dutch Java War of 1811. Raffles delegated a team to clear the site. Photographs from the late 19th century, however, show Borobudur in a poor state, with collapsed walls and slumped stupas. Countless statues had been removed: many were handed over to the King of Siam in 1896 and can now be seen in Bangkok. Only a massive restoration project lasting from 1968 to 1983 has turned Borobudur into the orderly, stable building we see today.

Now Borobudur is Indonesia's top tourist destination, bringing in 2.5 million visitors a year. It remains a monument of profound spiritual significance to Buddhists who come from all over the world each year to celebrate Vesak, 'Buddha's birthday'. Thousands of pilgrims join the ranks of monks in their yellow or orange-red robes, as they progress for 8 kilometres (5 miles) across the plain, passing two temples of the same age before reaching Borobudur in candlelight, chanting and releasing paper lanterns – scenes that might also have been familiar in Borobudur's heyday more than a thousand years ago.

EGYPT

SAUDI ARABIA

Jeddah

Mecca

Latitude 21°25'N **Longitude** 39°49'E

Location Central, western Saudi Arabia

Faith Muslim

Built After AD 630

Approximate area 850 square kilometres
(330 sq miles)

Access Only to Muslims, travelling with an
approved agency

MECCA

The Koran is not simply a historical account of the teachings of Islam: it is the word of God, vouchsafed in a series of divine revelations in Arabic to the Prophet Muhammad. They were first delivered to him in AD 610 in a cave high above the city of Mecca, where he liked to retreat to meditate.

Mecca, where Muhammad was born in about AD 570, was a prosperous trading centre. It was also a holy city, drawing pilgrims to the Black Stone, said to be a remnant of the first mosque built by the ancient patriarch Abraham. The stone was attached to a corner of a large stone cube called the Ka'aba, which contained numerous idols. The new religion of Islam was designed to sweep away such idolatry, and the confusion and corruption that went with it.

Muhammad spent over a decade in Mecca trying to promote Islam, before being driven out by its citizens. In AD 622 he fled with his family and followers to the city of Medina, 350 kilometres (220 miles) to the north, an event known as the Hijra, which marks the first year (1 AH) in the Islamic calendar. Here, Islam quickly gathered enough strength to challenge Mecca militarily. In AD 630, after a series of battles, Muhammad took Mecca. He died in Medina in AD 632, but already Islam had gathered military momentum, which saw it spread right across the Middle East, and across North Africa to southern Spain, within a century. Today it is the world's second largest faith.

Muhammad had declared Mecca the first city of Islam. The Ka'aba, emptied of its idols, became the primary focus of the

TRAVELLER'S TIPS

Best time to go: Any time of year is possible. But the main season is the Hajj, which takes place around the ninth day of Dhu al-Hijjah, which is the last month of the Islamic lunar year.

Look out for: Zamzam water: holy water from Hagar's spring in the Masjid al-Haram, brought home in large plastic jerry cans by pilgrims at the end of the Hajj.

Dos and don'ts: You cannot go to Mecca unless you are Muslim. Accreditation is usually done by licensed and approved travel agents.

The Masjid al-Haram is not only the holiest site in Islam; it is also the world's largest mosque; covering an area of more than 35 hectares (86 acres), it is capable of accommodating more than 2 million worshippers during the Hajj.

There are two storeys of arcaded galleries and extensive roof space around the central court of the mosque, capable of accommodating many thousands of worshippers. While the Masjid al-Haram originally dates from AD 638, after the death of Muhammad, it has been rebuilt numerous times, but the Ka'aba remains its pivotal point. The arcades were built between 1955 and 1973.

The Ka'aba is covered with a new black cloth called the Kiswah each year at the time of the Hajj. And each year it is cut into pieces and distributed among selected members of the faithful.

religion, to which all Muslims turn when they pray, wherever they are in the world. It is the focal point of the Masjid al-Haram, the largest and most important mosque of all. One of the 'Five Pillars of Islam' states that all Muslims should visit Mecca at least once in their lives, if they have the means and ability to do so. Today, more than 15 million pilgrims come to Mecca every year, most for the main annual pilgrimage called the Hajj.

The Hajj unfolds over several days, following ancient traditions. First the pilgrims – men dressed in their *ihram* of white towelling – enter the Masjid al-Haram and walk anticlockwise around the Ka'aba seven times. They drink the water from the Well of Zamzam, a spring that is said to have sprung up miraculously for Hagar, to save her infant Ishmael, son of Abraham. Then they head outside to walk or rush between two hillocks where Hagar ran in desperation to find water. The next day they go to the Plain of Arafat, 21 kilometres (13 miles) to the southeast, to pray and hear a sermon at the Mount of Mercy, where Muhammad delivered his farewell sermon; they perform standing prayers during the afternoon and watch the sun set. After this, they head back

towards Mecca to Muzdalifah, where they pray and gather pebbles to throw the following morning at one of three pillars representing the Devil at Mina; animals are sacrificed in memory of Abraham's sacrifice. More pebbles are thrown at the three pillars over the next two or three days before the Hajj is complete.

With the huge numbers involved, security and logistics are major challenges for Mecca – met with massive investment in recent years, funded by Saudi Arabia's oil wealth. Wahhabism, the dominant form of Islam in Saudi Arabia, is not sentimental about historical sites: they pose the risk of idolatry. Therefore most of the places connected with the life of the Prophet and his family and followers, including mosques and tombs, have been demolished. Modern buildings, meeting the needs of the pilgrimage, have taken their place – not the least of which is the new Mecca Royal Clock Tower Hotel, the world's second tallest building when completed in 2012, which now rises up over the Masjid al-Haram. Those wishing to visit the place of the inception of Islam, however, can still toil up the Jabal an-Nour (Mountain of Light) to visit Muhammad's cave.

PETRA

Latitude 31°19'N	**Longitude** 35°26'E
Location Southern Jordan	
Faith Nabataean, Roman, Christian	
Built c.3rd century BC to 7th century AD	
Approximate area 60 square kilometres (23 sq miles)	
Access 1, 2 and 3-day passes	

Isolation has always been Petra's trump card – isolation and determined human endeavour. Hidden away in a canyon that slashes through desert mountains, in ancient times it provided a natural refuge for the Nabataeans, who controlled the crossroads of trade routes across the Middle East, and garnered riches great enough to carve a magnificent city out of the living rock.

The drama of this setting has not diminished with time. Still the main access is the narrow ravine called the Siq, which winds downhill between towering cliffs before suddenly, theatrically, opening up to reveal a façade that looks like the entrance to some strange hybrid edifice: part-church, part-cave. Petra spreads out along a widening valley to the north, with temples and elaborate tombs gouged out of the golden sandstone cliff-faces on either side.

The city was inhabited for some 1,500 years, from around 400 BC. The Romans pushed into the region from the first century BC, bringing Roman gods and temples, and becoming Christian with the empire in the fourth century. The city declined when trade routes shifted and an earthquake struck Petra in AD 363.

After the rise and conquests of Islam in the seventh century, the Christian community of Petra became isolated, and it appealed for rescue to Baldwin I of Jerusalem at the end of the First Crusade, in around 1100. Petra then became a stronghold of the Crusaders, who embroidered legendary connections between Petra and the Biblical story of Moses on his journey to the Promised Land, pursued by the Pharaoh of Egypt. One of Petra's main water sources was the Wadi Musa (Valley of Moses), and its spring called Ein Musa (Well of Moses) is one of many sites where Moses is said to have followed God's instruction to strike a rock with his staff to find water miraculously in the desert.

The Nabataeans drew on their wide contacts with the Greeks, Egyptians and Assyrians to develop a distinctive architectural style of their own for their most impressive rock-hewn buildings, such as Al-Deir (The Monastery).

In contrast to the architectural sophistication of some of the façades, the interior spaces are by and large unadorned. In many cases, their creators seem simply to have extrapolated forms from the natural shapes in the rocks.

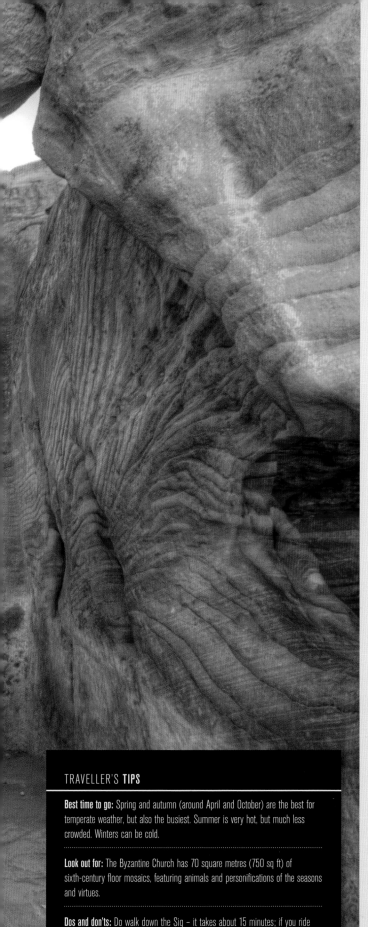

Petra was abandoned after the Crusades, visited only by Bedouin herders who brought their flocks to feed on scrub and drink from the springs; they used the rock-carved tombs to store winter fodder. Nonetheless, the legends survived in the Arabic names (Moses is, after all, revered as a prophet in Islam). So what was perhaps the royal mausoleum of the Nabataean king Aretas IV now took the name Al-Khazneh al-Faroun ('The Pharaoh's Treasury', or simply 'The Treasury'). The city's main temple, probably dedicated to the Nabataeans' chief male god Dushara, is called Qasr Bint al-Faroun ('House of the Pharaoh's Daughter'). The name of the large Nabataean rock-carved tomb called Al-Deir ('The Monastery'), in the hills 1 kilometre (0.6 miles) above the city, is probably more historically accurate, reflecting its use by Christian monks.

Centuries later, in 1812, a 27-year-old Swiss explorer and Arabist called Johann Ludwig Burckhardt – travelling furtively in Arab disguise – stumbled upon the ruins, and guessed that this was the Petra mentioned in ancient records. His reports inspired a romantic vision of a lost city, the 'rose-red city – half as old as time' as the poet John William Burgon famously put it in 1845, having never set eyes on it. The trickle of European visitors gathered momentum. Now Petra is Jordan's top tourist attraction, receiving some 6,000 visitors a day.

Like the strange striations of colour in the rock faces, history and successive religions have been layered into the fabric of Petra. Much mystery surrounds it still, and the rocks remain mute, yielding their story only in incremental, hard-won archaeological deductions, but haunting departing visitors with their beauty.

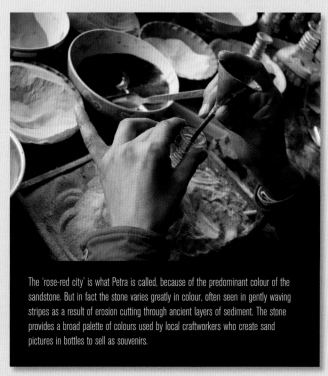

The 'rose-red city' is what Petra is called, because of the predominant colour of the sandstone. But in fact the stone varies greatly in colour, often seen in gently waving stripes as a result of erosion cutting through ancient layers of sediment. The stone provides a broad palette of colours used by local craftworkers who create sand pictures in bottles to sell as souvenirs.

TRAVELLER'S TIPS

Best time to go: Spring and autumn (around April and October) are the best for temperate weather, but also the busiest. Summer is very hot, but much less crowded. Winters can be cold.

Look out for: The Byzantine Church has 70 square metres (750 sq ft) of sixth-century floor mosaics, featuring animals and personifications of the seasons and virtues.

Dos and don'ts: Do walk down the Siq – it takes about 15 minutes; if you ride (horse, donkey or buggy), you'll miss the sites along the way, and some of the unfolding drama.

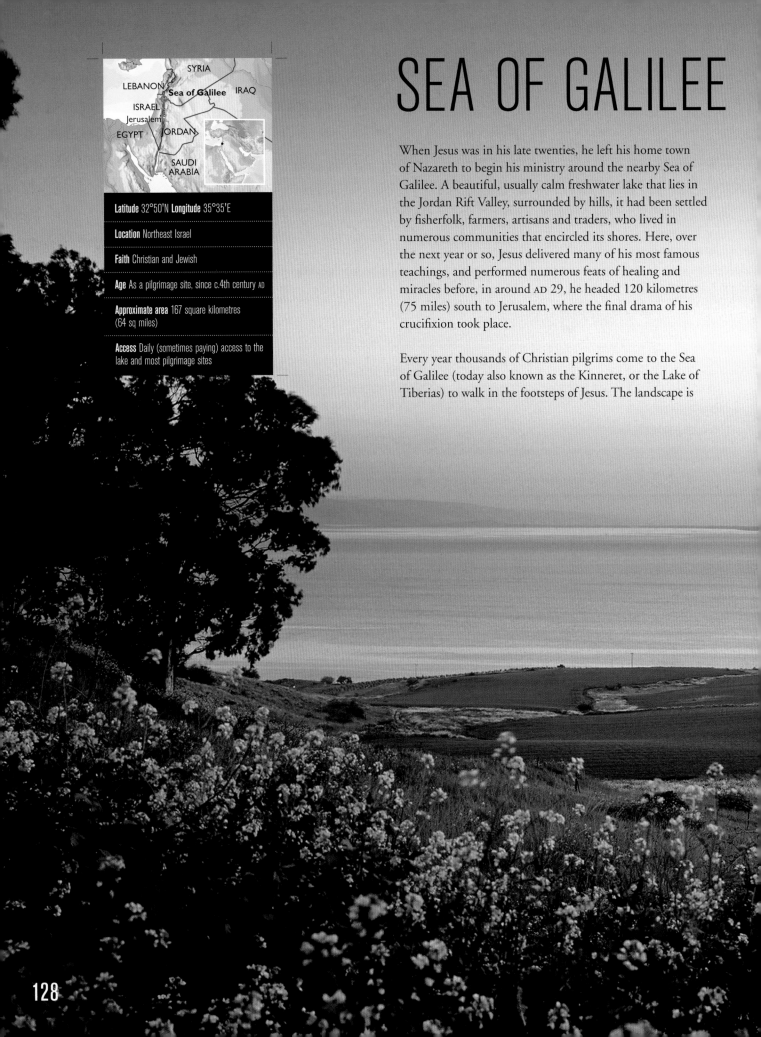

SEA OF GALILEE

Latitude 32°50'N **Longitude** 35°35'E	
Location Northeast Israel	
Faith Christian and Jewish	
Age As a pilgrimage site, since c.4th century AD	
Approximate area 167 square kilometres (64 sq miles)	
Access Daily (sometimes paying) access to the lake and most pilgrimage sites	

When Jesus was in his late twenties, he left his home town of Nazareth to begin his ministry around the nearby Sea of Galilee. A beautiful, usually calm freshwater lake that lies in the Jordan Rift Valley, surrounded by hills, it had been settled by fisherfolk, farmers, artisans and traders, who lived in numerous communities that encircled its shores. Here, over the next year or so, Jesus delivered many of his most famous teachings, and performed numerous feats of healing and miracles before, in around AD 29, he headed 120 kilometres (75 miles) south to Jerusalem, where the final drama of his crucifixion took place.

Every year thousands of Christian pilgrims come to the Sea of Galilee (today also known as the Kinneret, or the Lake of Tiberias) to walk in the footsteps of Jesus. The landscape is punctuated with memories of New Testament stories: for instance, nearby is Tabgha where Jesus is believed to have performed the miracle of the Feeding of the 5,000, with just five loaves and two fishes. Out on the lake itself, Jesus miraculously walked upon water and calmed a storm when travelling in a boat with his panicked disciples.

But the Sea of Galilee is not uniquely a place of Christian pilgrimage. Tiberias is one of the Four Holy Cities of Judaism and served as a refuge for the Jews after the Second Jewish Revolt against the Romans and their expulsion from Jerusalem in AD 135. Pilgrims are drawn above all to the tomb of the great Jewish sage Maimonides, known as Rambam, physician to the Muslim ruler Saladin, who was buried here after his death in Cairo in 1204.

The view south near the ruins of Capernaum will have changed little since Christ's time, when the town – home to several of the disciples – became a headquarters for the new faith.

Sunlight sparkles on the dome and warms the stone of one of the eight sets of archways at the head of steps that lead up to the platform on which the Dome of the Rock rests.

DOME OF THE ROCK

Latitude 31°7'N **Longitude** 35°23'E
Location Jerusalem, Israel
Faith Islam
Built AD 685–91
Approximate area Temple Mount: 14 hectares (35 acres)
Access Temple Mount is accessible to all, but usually only Muslims can enter the Dome and Al-Aqsa Mosque

The most prominent landmark of Old Jerusalem – sacred city to Jews, Christians and Muslims alike – is one of the most beautiful of all Islamic buildings, a simple octagon decorated with delicate tilework and topped by a golden dome that catches the brilliant Middle Eastern sunlight. It stands over a natural feature of colossal symbolic power and spiritual resonance: the Rock is the craggy summit of a limestone hill that many Orthodox Jews believe to be the Foundation Stone, where heaven and earth meet, where God created both the earth and Adam. A cavern beneath it, visible through a round hole, is said to be the Well of Souls, in which can be heard the voices of the Dead mixed with the sound of the Rivers of Paradise. The Rock is also where Abraham brought his son Isaac to offer him as a sacrifice to God.

Around the summit the Jews built their Temple, the first under King Solomon, in 957 BC. After its destruction by the Babylonians, a second Temple was built in 516 BC. This in turn was destroyed by the Romans in AD 70, and, after the revolt of 132–5 AD, the Jews were largely dispersed abroad. The Ark of the Covenant was said to have rested on the Rock in the Holy of Holies of the First Temple, making the site so sacred that observant Jews are forbidden to approach it: the nearest they can come to it is now the Western Wall (the 'Wailing Wall'), the last remnant of the old Temple.

The Rock is sacred also to Muslims. In about AD 621, during a mystical episode called the 'Night Journey', the Prophet Muhammed was visited by the Archangel Gabriel in Mecca, who brought him the heavenly steed of the prophets, Al-Buraq ('Lightning') to ride, and together they travelled through the

132

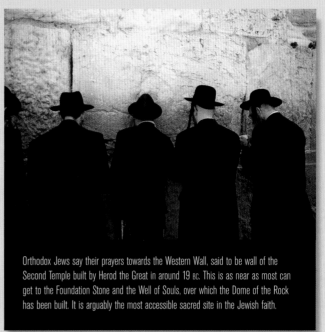

Orthodox Jews say their prayers towards the Western Wall, said to be wall of the Second Temple built by Herod the Great in around 19 BC. This is as near as most can get to the Foundation Stone and the Well of Souls, over which the Dome of the Rock has been built. It is arguably the most accessible sacred site in the Jewish faith.

night sky to Jerusalem. Here – from the Rock embedded in the flat, artificial plinth of Temple Mount, according to some traditions – Muhammed climbed a ladder of golden light through the seven heavens, finally entering the presence of Allah, who told him that Muslims are permitted to pray just five times a day; Muhammed descended and returned to Mecca that same night. Jerusalem thereafter became Sunni Islam's third most sacred city, after Mecca and Medina.

In AD 634 the Muslims captured the predominantly Christian city of Jerusalem, and in AD 685 – just 64 years or so after the Night Journey – Caliph Abd al-Malik initiated work on a shrine over the Rock. The architecture is essentially Byzantine, with classical pillars and arches, crowned by a dome 20 metres (66 ft) in diameter; but the geometric decoration is Islamic. The dome and arches, richly inlaid with gilding, tilework and Koranic inscriptions, create an airy open space over the centrepiece: a contrastingly raw, bare and craggy slab of rock.

In recent decades, the Dome of the Rock has become a defiantly Islamic landmark in a contested city. It forms part of a protected enclave called the Noble Sanctuary, which it shares with the equally revered Al-Aqsa Mosque. Access, controlled by the age-old Islamic Waqf (Authority), is tightly regulated. In the past, the dome was sheathed in lead, then an aluminium and bronze alloy. In 1993 it was coated in gold, focusing eyes and minds on a symbol of both the intense spirituality and the bitter contentions of this Holy Land.

The decorative tiles on the outside of the Dome of the Rock date from the 16th-century Ottoman era, when the building was restored on the orders of Suleiman the Magnificent.

BLUE MOSQUE

The Sultan Ahmet Mosque is known as the Blue Mosque because that is the predominant colour of its interior – a gorgeous soft blue, the cumulative effect of the 20,000 tiles that line the walls and arches. In detail, they are not simply blue at all, but intricate arabesques of flowers, vines, trees, Arabic calligraphy and geometric patterns that introduce white, red, green and brown. Higher up, the domes and semi-domes of the ceilings are painted and gilded with patterns in a similar palette.

Daylight flows in through ranks of 260 windows, some of them filtering colour through stained glass. The floor is covered with wall-to-wall carpet, muffling the sound and feeling warmly soft. Giant flat wheels of chandeliers, slung low overhead, glimmer like candles. The result is a canopy of startling beauty – a symphony of arched space that welcomes worshippers and visitors alike into its embrace, inviting them to prayer or quiet contemplation.

This was the grand project of Sultan Ahmet I, who came to the throne of the Ottoman Empire at the age of just 13 in 1603. His aim was to build a mosque in Ottoman style

The multi-domed ceiling is kaleidoscopic in its effect, sparkling with delicate and multicoloured tilework. The ranks of clear windows that surround the dome let in enough natural light to allow the mood of the mosque to change with the weather and the hour of the day, sometimes softly muted and golden, sometimes pierced with beams of sunlight. In the evening the ceiling is illuminated from inside with uplights.

The Blue Mosque has a commanding view over the Bosphorus, close to the fabled tip of Old Istanbul, which has been known since ancient times as the Golden Horn.

Istanbul

TURKEY

CYPRUS

Latitude 41°0'N **Longitude** 28°58'E

Location Istanbul, Turkey

Faith Muslim

Built 1609–16

Approximate area 9,000 square metres (96,900 sq ft)

Access Free access daily; closed to non-worshippers during prayers

that would outshine the magnificent Hagia Sophia, the 'Church of Holy Wisdom' that stands just 300 metres (330 yards) to the northeast. Hagia Sophia had been built as a Christian place of worship by the Byzantine Emperor Justinian more than 1,000 years before; it had been converted into a mosque after the Ottoman conquest of Istanbul (or Constantinople, as it then was) in 1453.

Ottoman architecture, which combined Byzantine style and engineering with Islamic principles, had reached a peak with Mimar Sinan (c.1490–1588), chief architect to Suleiman the Magnificent. Sultan Ahmet I chose one of Sinan's pupils, Sedefkar Mehmet Agha (c.1540–1617), to undertake his mosque, and work began in 1609. Mehmet Agha followed very much in Sinan's footsteps: there are many similarities with the Süleymaniye Mosque in Istanbul, which Sinan built for Suleiman the Magnificent. In both, a cluster of domes and semi-domes around the main central dome forms the body of the mosque, ingeniously carving out the interior space. Attached to this is a large, open courtyard, framed by high arcades with domed ceilings. At the Blue Mosque there are four tall, spired minarets at each corner of the mosque, and two additional, slightly smaller ones at the far corners of the courtyard: six in all. This proved controversial, as it matched the number of minarets of Islam's holiest shrine, the Grand Mosque, or Masjid al-Haram, of Mecca. To counter criticism, Sultan Ahmet had to send Mehmet Agha to Mecca to build a seventh minaret.

The Blue Mosque's silhouette of cascading domes and its six minarets, set on high ground above the Sea of Marmara, forms one of the great landmarks of Istanbul. But it is really the interior that justifies its reputation as one of the world's most beautiful mosques. The town of Iznik, to the southeast of Istanbul, where the tiles were made, had produced ceramics and tiles for the whole of the Ottoman Empire. The original inspiration for its style had been rare blue-and-white porcelain from China, which the Ottomans had imported since the 14th century. Iznik tiles had developed a sophistication of their own – but came at a high price. No matter: Sultan Ahmet's mosque was as extravagant as it was large.

He was not able to enjoy it for long. In 1617, just one year after the Blue Mosque was completed, Sultan Ahmet I died of typhus, aged 27. Mehmet Agha died that same year. It was left to future sultans and their families to immerse themselves in the exquisite beauty of the interior – just as thousands of visitors are able to do today, four centuries later.

The clustered dome construction creates a huge, airy space inside, tempered by the intricate patterning and the stained-glass windows, which help to give it a human scale.

MOUNT ARARAT

Latitude 39°42'N **Longitude** 44°17'E	
Location Eastern Turkey	
Faith Pagan, Jewish, Christian, Muslim	
Age Volcanically active in 3rd century BC	
Approximate area 1,000 square kilometres (400 sq miles)	
Access With an official permit and a certified guide only	

Turkey's highest mountain is a spectacular dormant volcano, a double peak soaring out of the remote and dusty plains at its far eastern fringes, close to its border with Iran and Armenia, to reach its permanently snow-covered summit at 5,137 metres (16,854 ft). Is this the place where God gave humankind its second chance?

The early chapters of the Book of Genesis in the Bible tell how God was so incensed by the 'wickedness of man' that he regretted their creation, and decided to destroy his work in a Great Flood. Only Noah and his family were selected to survive, tipped off by God to build an Ark of wood in which they, and pairs of all animals, could float above the

TRAVELLER'S **TIPS**

Best time to go: The climbing season is July to mid-September (late summer). Most favourable of all is late August. The region is snow-bound in winter.

Look out for: The Turkish town of Dogubeyazit is famous for its giant meatballs called *abdigör köfte*, found only here. Served with rice, one is usually sufficient.

Dos and don'ts: Don't try to climb Mount Ararat without an official permit. This is available through the Ministry of Tourism, or through licensed trekking companies.

The classic Armenian view of Mount Ararat includes the monastery of Khor Virap, associated with St Gregory the Illuminator.

floodwaters, which rose for 40 days and nights. Finally the flood receded, and after 150 days the Ark came to rest on 'the mountains of Ararat'; the world could now be repopulated from this new beginning.

For centuries the supposed wreckage of the Ark has been spotted on the flanks of Mount Ararat, particularly among the ice-fields and glaciers close to the lava-encrusted summit – the only place where such ancient timber could conceivably survive. Boat-like shapes have been identified, notably the 'Ararat Anomaly', 2.2 kilometres (1.4 miles) to the west of the summit, photographed numerous times from the air and from satellites since 1949. Evidence on the ground is even more elusive, but in 2007 fossilized wooden beams were found by evangelical Christian explorers in ice caves high on the mountain's flanks. The world at large, however, has remained unconvinced, suggesting that rock and ice formations and hoaxes are more likely explanations. In Muslim tradition, the Ark alighted on Mount Judi, but its location is uncertain.

None of this diminishes the sanctity of Mount Ararat – above all to the Armenians. Although the Armenians were the first to adopt Christianity as their national religion, in AD 301, they

A large number of the people living on the Turkish side of Mount Ararat are Kurds. They live by farming and herding, and their dwellings are often little more than small stone huts. Kurdish lands traditionally spread across the borders of Turkey, Syria, Iraq and Iran. During the 1920s, the Kurds proclaimed a Republic of Ararat in southeastern Turkey, but it was crushed by the Turkish army in 1930.

still refer to Mount Ararat at the 'home of the gods', and of their supreme pre-Christian deity called Ara. In the past, Mount Ararat lay within the boundaries of Greater Armenia, but in 1921 the borders were redrawn, and Mount Ararat became a part of Turkey, its peaks rising tantalizingly just 32 kilometres (20 miles) from the frontier, and visible from the capital, Yerevan. The Armenians view this as an injustice closely associated with the massacres carried out by the Ottoman Turks across the region between 1915 and 1923. While Armenia was under Soviet domination, from 1920 to 1990, Cold War antagonism closed off the mountain, and even now access is restricted. This serves only to intensify Mount Ararat's bittersweet status as a sacred mountain. It is close to the Armenian soul, and a symbol of the motherland: it appears on the Armenian coat of arms, on banknotes and stamps and is the subject of paintings, poems and songs.

One of the best views of the two peaks is from Khor Virap, a monastery of the Armenian Apostolic Church dating from the seventh century, built on the hill site of a prison in the ancient capital of Greater Armenia, Artashat, where St Gregory the Illuminator, patron saint of Armenia, had been imprisoned for some 13 years. Here Armenian Christianity, nationhood and deep biblical history are linked in a single frame. But the unequivocal majesty of the mountain itself transcends any prism through which it might be viewed.

An evocative, part-ruined palace and mosque, near the Turkish town of Dogubeyazit, command a spectacular view across a wide plain to Mount Ararat. They were built in the 18th century by a local Ottoman ruler called Ishak Pasha.

GÖREME, CAPPADOCIA

Latitude 38°40'N **Longitude** 34°50'E	
Location Central Turkey	
Faith Christian (now Muslim)	
Built From c.6th century to 13th century	
Approximate area 120 square kilometres (46 sq miles)	
Access Ticketed entry to Göreme Open Air Museum, daily	

The dream-like, other-worldly landscape of central Cappadocia is a place of wonder. Some 30 million years ago, three volcanoes spewed out a sea of ash and the occasional hard basalt boulder that, over the millennia, have eroded away to form rippling cliffs, and spires known as 'fairy chimneys'. The compacted tufa rock is soft enough to carve, so – instead of building – local people have been gouging out homes, stables and storerooms from at least Hittite times in around 1800 BC. They also created extensive underground 'cities', several storeys deep, capable of hiding perhaps 4,000 people when under attack or siege – and so secret that they have only been rediscovered since the 1960s.

The secrecy of this often labyrinthine landscape has played a central role in its history. Although close to high-value trade routes linking East to West across Turkey, central Cappadocia was hard to penetrate and to conquer. An independent kingdom from about 600 BC, Cappadocia became a Roman province in AD 17, but was never heavily Romanized. It did, however, receive a visit from St Paul, and adopted Christianity with enthusiasm.

Early Christians could hide among the fairy chimneys to avoid the three centuries of persecutions that followed. When the Roman Empire turned Christian in the fourth century, Cappadocia became a centre of monasticism: St Basil the Great, a founding figure of the Eastern Orthodox Church and its traditions of monasticism, was the Bishop of Caesarea, now Kayseri, the principal city of the region.

Between the 6th and 13th centuries, dozens of small, intimate churches and chapels were carved out of the soft tufa rock, most notably in the Göreme Valley (and now protected within the boundaries of the Göreme Open Air Museum). Often hidden away in canyons and accessed by ladders or flights of steps to positions high on a cliff-face, the unadorned façades of bare rock give no hint of the elaborate churches inside, with their columns, arches, barrel vaulting and domes richly

A cave in the Rose Valley near Cavusin, named for its striking coloration. This was used as a home, but the potential for creating more elaborate interior space was exploited nearby in two rock-hewn churches, Ayvali and Haçli (Church of the Cross).

At their most extreme, the forces of erosion and the contrasting strata of rock have created 'fairy chimneys', crowned by gnome-like caps.

decorated with murals in finest Byzantine style – pictures of biblical scenes and the saints in colours vividly preserved in the absence of light.

Many of these rock-cut churches have poetic names taken from a particular feature. The Church of the Snake, for instance, derives its name from a picture of St George slaying a snake-like dragon. The Church of the Apple may refer to a red orb held by the Archangel Michael in a mural, or perhaps apple trees that once stood outside the entrance. The Church of the Sandals refers to impressions in the rock said to have been cast from footprints of Jesus in Jerusalem. The Church of Buckle – the largest in Göreme – was named after a decorative feature that has since disappeared.

The Göreme churches belonged to a complex of monasteries. One of the best preserved is the Nunnery, a warren on about six floors excavated out of a rock pile resembling a castle of dribbled sand on a beach. It has cells, a dining hall and kitchen, a chapel and a church decorated with simple geometric murals. 'Millstone doors' could be rolled across internal tunnels to block off access in times of danger, a feature also of the underground 'cities' – and a reminder of the precarious times as the Byzantine Empire tottered to its close. After the 12th century Cappadocia fell victim to raids by first the Seljuks and then the Ottoman Turks. The Ottomans completed their conquest of the Byzantine Empire with the Fall of Constantinople in 1453, and Turkey became Muslim. The Christians of Cappadocia either converted or fled; their churches and monasteries were abandoned, and many were turned over to secular use, such as stabling. But enough have survived to provide one of Christianity's most curious and enchanting legacies.

TRAVELLER'S TIPS

Best time to go: Spring through to the autumn is good; winter can be chilly and snow-covered. In mid-summer, arrive early at the Open Air Museum to avoid the crowds and heat.

Look out for: In many of the churches at Göreme, the eyes in the paintings low down have been scratched out. This was apparently done since Christian times to avert the 'evil eye' that might bring misfortune.

Dos and don'ts: Do visit one of the mysterious underground 'cities', used for centuries but abandoned after the Christian era; the largest are at Derinkuyu, Kaymakli (south of Göreme) and Özkonak (to the north).

Many of the homes in Göreme village are made in the same strange way as the nearby churches: by carving spaces out of the soft rock. The whole village is backed by high cliffs that shield it like a cupped hand.

SAMARKAND

'If Paradise can be found in this world, then Samarkand is it,' wrote the 13th-century Persian historian Ata-Malek Juvayni. This ancient city, founded perhaps 2,500 years ago, prospered from its well-irrigated land and its location on the Silk Road, the trans-Asian trade routes that brought precious goods – silk, gemstones, porcelain, tea, paper, spices – all the way from China to the Mediterranean world of the Romans, Byzantines and the Renaissance. It was the Mongol era that finally put an end to that trade, and in 1220 Genghis Khan sacked the city that Juvayni so praised. But exactly 150 years later, his Muslim successor in spirit Timur, or Tamerlane, brought a new glory to Samarkand when he made it his capital.

Tamerlane was a merciless conqueror, but he loved fine architecture, and drew from his conquered lands the very best architects, artists and craftsmen. This was a golden age of Islamic design and architecture, with elegant arches, domes and minarets adorned with delicate, brilliant tilework. Tamerlane's own Gur-e Amir mausoleum in Samarkand is an exquisite example of this. Better was yet to come. The glory of Samarkand is its central square, the Registan ('Sandy Place'), built in the 15th and 17th centuries. Three large madrassahs (religious schools) face each other across a wide plaza, each with intricately decorated façades with a high-arched entrance hall, or *irwan*. Few other cultures in the world have applied such colour and lavish artistic design to the exterior of their buildings, all underpinned by glorious blues.

There is much more, including the extraordinary Shakhi-Zinda necropolis, with its 20 elaborate mausoleums and 40 tombs, dating from the 9th to 19th centuries. All the finest buildings of Samarkand are religious, and rank among the world's most eloquent architectural expressions of the refined aspirations and serenity of devotion.

Latitude 39°39'N **Longitude** 66°57'E	
Location Eastern Uzbekistan	
Faith Muslim	
Built From the 9th century	
Approximate area 10 square kilometres (4 sq miles)	
Access Daily; some sites require tickets	

Registan Square – with its three intricately tiled madrasahs – is one of the world's most beautiful town centres.

TRAVELLER'S TIPS

Best time to go: Spring (mid-March to end May) or autumn (September to early November) are both good.

Look out for: In Samarkand's ruined ancient city of Afrosiab is a mausoleum with an 18-metre (60-ft) tomb supposedly containing the biblical prophet Daniel, brought by Tamerlane from Syria.

Dos and don'ts: Do buy some Samarkand *non* bread, which is a traditional gift to travel with. It is made in thick disks, with printed and coloured decorations, and can last up to three years.

KARNAK

Latitude 25°43'N **Longitude** 32°39'E	
Location Luxor, southern Egypt	
Faith Ancient Egyptian	
Built From c.1950 BC	
Approximate area 40 hectares (100 acres)	
Access Ticketed entry, daily	

Karnak was the great state temple of ancient Egypt. Its scale is deliberately, crushingly gigantic: processional ways lined by dozens of sphinxes, massive pylon gateways leading to vast open courtyards and then to halls crowded with forests of columns, tattooed with hundreds of hieroglyphic engravings. This is a whirlwind tour of 2,000 years of history, with a roll-call of many of the most famous and powerful pharaohs, each attached to devotional shrines, obelisks and statues, as well as to illustrated accounts glorifying their achievements and immortalizing their intense relationships with Egypt's complex pantheon of gods.

Karnak flourished when Thebes (now Luxor) was the capital of Egypt, and of an empire that spanned the Middle

East. Power had shifted to here in about 2040 BC, after a period of turmoil put an end to the pyramid-building Old Kingdom based in the former capital of Memphis (near to modern Cairo). The kings of Thebes, the new pharaohs, were an incarnation of their local god of fecundity, Amun, now seen in combination with the old supreme deity of Egypt, the sun-god Re.

Thebes was not just a capital, but a physical image of the cosmos. Running through it from south to north was the sacred River Nile, volatile giver of life, source of water and fertility to the rich ribbon of agricultural land that sustained the nation. On its eastern banks, the side of the sunrise and life, stood Karnak, and the smaller Temple of Luxor. To the

west were the rocky hills where the sun set, and where the kings and queens were buried in lavish tombs to begin their journeys into the afterlife. Each day Amun-Re, the sun god, progressed across the sky from east to west in his barque, before re-entering the Underworld. It was the task of the temples, and their great armies of priests, to maintain this sacred order through to correct conduct of daily ritual.

Karnak, in common with other ancient Egyptian temples, was not a place of public worship; it was the terrestrial home of the gods, represented by statues, which only the pharaohs

The calm of the Sacred Lake, where priests would purify themselves in holy water, contrasts with the complexity of the ruins.

TRAVELLER'S **TIPS**

Best time to go: The cool season, November to April. Summer temperatures regularly reach 40°C (104°F). It very rarely rains in Luxor.

Look out for: The Karnak Sound and Light show is performed three times every night, at hourly intervals, in various languages following a weekly schedule.

Dos and don'ts: Go as early as possible in the day to avoid the crowds. It's a huge site: allow plenty of time, and take water.

A large stone sculpture of a scarab beetle stands next to the Sacred Lake. Scarabs were worshipped because of their habit of rolling balls of dung, seen as symbols of the earth, which was renewed daily by Khepri, god of the rising sun.

themselves, or highest priests, could approach. The main focus of Karnak was the Precinct of Amun, where the god was worshipped as part of the Theban Triad, which also included his wife Mut, and their son Khonsu.

The precinct also contains the temples of both Seti II and Ramses III; the Great Festival Hall built by the warrior king Tuthmosis III; and temples to Khonsu, and to Opet, the hippopotamus-headed goddess of Thebes. The Sacred Lake was used by priests to conduct their daily ablutions: cleanliness was essential to their task. Just to the north is the Precinct of Montu, the falcon-headed warrior god; and to the south, linked by a processional way lined by sphinxes, is the Precinct of Mut, with a set of large black granite statues of the lion-headed warrior goddess Sekhmet overlooking the court. A further processional way, also lined with sphinxes, once led to the Temple of Luxor, 3 kilometres (2 miles) to the south.

But the two temples were more famously linked by water in the great annual Festival of Opet – the only occasion when the public could pay direct tribute to Amun and the Theban Triad. After the annual flooding of the River Nile – greeted as a blessing, a rebirth, and a renewal of their favours – the three gods were taken in their sacred barques at Karnak and placed on barges. Then, in a massive regal procession accompanied by priests, dancers, acrobats and musicians, the barges were towed upriver to visit the Temple of Luxor, an occasion for wild partying that lasted a full month. A series of relief sculptures at Karnak records the festivities, which were celebrated for at least 700 years.

The towering obelisk of Queen Hatshepsut, one of a pair, dominates the site, here viewed from beside the columns of the Great Hypostyle Hall. Obelisks were said to represent a ray of the sun, and to channel its power.

MOUNT SINAI

Latitude 28°33'N **Longitude** 35°58'E	
Location Southern Sinai, Egypt	
Faith Christian (Eastern Orthodox)	
Built From the 6th century AD	
Approximate area 4,200 square metres (45,210 sq ft)	
Access Ticketed entry, limited access within the monastery	

Camels seen winding their way across the valley floor underline the scale and bone-dry desolation of Mount Sinai, which rises to its craggy peak to the rear.

The route from Egypt to the promised land of Canaan lies through the triangular peninsula of Sinai. In this desolate and empty place, according to the book of Exodus, the tribes of Israel wandered for 40 years after their escape from Pharaoh. At the start of that nomadic time, Moses ascended a mountain to receive the Ten Commandments directly from God. 'Mount Sinai was altogether on a smoke, because the Lord descended upon it in fire,' says the Bible, 'And the whole mount quaked greatly.'

There are many candidates for the precise site of that momentous mountaintop encounter between God and Moses.

But by longstanding tradition, the name Mount Sinai is given to the peak close to where the monastery of St Catherine now stands. It is named after St Catherine of Alexandria, the fourth-century Christian martyr who, so the legend goes, was due to be tortured to death by the Romans on a spiked wheel, but the wheel miraculously disintegrated (hence the name of the firework called the Catherine wheel) – so she was beheaded instead. Her body was taken by angels to the peak of Mount Sinai for burial.

This is what an imagined monastery might look like – the ultimate refuge in a hostile world. An oasis surrounded by the

TRAVELLER'S TIPS

Best time to go: In the winter months, between November and April (but it can be cold). Note that the monastery is open from 9 a.m. to noon only, and closed on Friday and Sunday.

Look out for: The tree-like bramble at the Chapel of the Burning Bush is the original 'burning bush', or a cutting from it, according to local tradition.

Dos and don'ts: Do set out early for the climb, which takes two to three hours, to catch the sunrise. Take water, hats and sun protection.

harsh and unforgiving desert, it was originally built in AD 548–67. Still inhabited by 22 Eastern Orthodox monks, it is one of the world's oldest Christian monasteries in continuous use. Today, its visitors are primarily tourists, but it has been the focus of pilgrimage for more than 1,000 years. It has survived in a Muslim land because – so it is claimed – it is protected by a decree, called the Achtiname, forbidding any act that might harm the monks; this was dictated by the Prophet Muhammad himself, who, according to a local tradition, actually visited the monastery. Indeed, St Catherine's Monastery is often held up as a model of cooperation between the faiths, maintained over the centuries: it even contains a small 12th-century mosque within its walls.

So Mount Sinai is a sacred place for Jews, Christians and Muslims alike, not least because Moses is a patriarch to all three religions. Early Christian hermits lived in this mountainous desert region to escape persecution by the Romans. Their communities coalesced to form primitive monasteries, which became increasingly troubled by marauders. Early in his reign as Byzantine emperor, they

petitioned Justinian I for protection, and he duly built a fortified monastery for them at Mount Sinai. In Arabic the mountain is known as Jebel Musa (Mountain of Moses), which seems to corroborate its identity – or at least to hint at an inter-faith consensus.

Because the monastery houses the supposed relics of St Catherine, it became a place of pilgrimage. Most of the monastery today dates from after the 12th century: the high walls were built in the 17th century, for instance. Within their protective embrace, there are treasures to match the monastery's great age. Its main Church of St Catherine contains a glittering sixth-century Byzantine mosaic illustrating the Transfiguration of Christ (the miracle in which Jesus becomes suffused with radiant light and appears with Moses and the Prophet Elijah before three of his Apostles). The monastery also has a collection of more than 2,000 precious icons, some painted as long ago as the fifth century. The library contains one of the biggest and most important collections of Christian manuscripts in the world, second only to the Vatican library.

The Charnel House or Ossuary of St Catherine's Monastery, outside its main walls, is the object of fascination for visitors. In common with the burial practices found at other Eastern Orthodox monasteries, the bodies of monks were first buried and later exhumed. The public display of their bones is said to bring spiritual benefit as a reminder of the vanity and transience of human life.

The monastery and the Biblical landscape that surrounds it resonate with history and legend stretching back more than 3,000 years. There is a message for all humanity here, which deserves our respect and protection – as the Achtiname of Muhammad declares.

There is a simple Eastern Orthodox Christian chapel on the summit of Mount Sinai, as well as a small mosque – but the landscape is the most eloquent expression of the religious significance of the site.

LALIBELA

This is not building, this is sculpture – and on the grandest scale. Some 800 years ago the Christian inhabitants of Roha (now Lalibela) decided to excavate the red, volcanic crust of their high, undulating countryside to create a set of 11 rock churches, in three groups, linked by underground passages. It was a feat of extraordinary endeavour, in a remote corner of Christendom, which stunned the first Europeans explorers who came upon it in the 1520s – a Portuguese party led by Pêro da Covilhã.

The churches are richly decorated inside with murals depicting the Virgin Mary and stories of the Bible; with engraved geometric patterns around the arches, often picked out in colour; with bas relief sculptures of the saints; with brightly coloured textile hangings – all bearing the patina of long use, redolent with frankincense, and dingy in the candlelight and the muted daylight that filters through the rock-cut window apertures. Centuries of meditation and prayer have left their imprint in the undisturbed silence. But it is the exteriors of these buildings that explain the awe in which they are held. Their creators could have sculpted them in any shape, but instead they replicate the neat, hard-edged lines and flat façades of built churches – in vivid contrast to the flanks of their rough-hewn pits from which they stand free. But some liberties in design have been taken, such as the window shapes: Bet Medhane Alem (House of the Saviour of the World) has keyhole-shaped windows; Bet Mariam (House of the Virgin Mary) has crosses and swastikas.

There is no clear explanation why these churches were created in this way – apart from the fact that the landscape permitted it. Architecturally they bear no relation to the local, traditional domestic buildings, which are stone-built cylinders crowned by shallow, conical thatch. The churches are believed to date from the time of the king and saint Gebre Meskel Lalibela (ruled from about 1181 to 1221), whose Christian kingdom survived the fall of the Axum Empire, which had dominated the region since the third century BC. Through trade with Syria and Palestine, and contact with Coptic Egypt to the north, Axum had been Christian since the fourth century.

Lalibela made his capital at Roha and it was renamed in his honour. It is said that he had travelled to Jerusalem on a

---

The cruciform shape of Bet Giyorgis is clear from the surface. Its relatively small pit leaves it virtually subterranean.

Latitude 12°2'N Longitude 39°2'E

Location North central Ethiopia

Faith Christian (Ethiopian Orthodox)

Built Probably 12th and 13th centuries

Approximate area 12 hectares (30 acres)

Access Ticketed access for foreign visitors, open daily

TRAVELLER'S TIPS

Best time to go: Time your visit to coincide with a festival. Otherwise go in the dry season (October to March). The churches may be closed during the wettest part of the rainy season (June–September).

Look out for: Pilgrims collecting small handfuls of soil from around the churches. It is said to have the miraculous power to cure disease.

Dos and don'ts: Do hire a licensed guide, whose local knowledge will be invaluable. The churches are dark: take a torch.

The creators of the churches took advantage of the soft rock to decorate the interiors with bas relief carvings, as seen in this image of a saint at Bet Golgotha. Across the site, landmarks and structures are said to represent locations from the story of Christ, such as the stable where he was born and the River Jordan where he was baptized.

pilgrimage as a young man (or saw it in a vision), but after the Muslim leader Saladin seized the city from the Crusaders in 1187, impeding pilgrimage for Ethiopians, Lalibela decided (or was instructed by St George in a dream) to reproduce a 'New Jerusalem' in his capital. Some researchers, however, have argued that the churches may be much older than this.

Today Lalibela is a small town of 14,500 inhabitants, who benefit from the income of a steady stream of tourists. But it really comes to life at the festivals, notably Christmas or Ledet (7 January in the calendar of the Ethiopian Orthodox Church), Epiphany or Timkat (19 January), Easter or Fasika, and Meskel, the Festival of the Cross, which marks the beginning of spring. Tens of thousands of pilgrims converge on the town in a sea of long white robes and turbans, punctuated by robes in primary colours. Hundreds of priests gather for the ceremonies, sheltering beneath elaborate parasols, wearing colourful robes and turbans or gilt-embroidered cylindrical hats. The crowds chant and sway in ranks, in an escalating fervour of devotion. Priests perform exorcisms; miracle cures are acclaimed. And in quieter daylight moments the pilgrims stand on the rims of the excavated pits, gazing down in awe at the churches, and stream through the rock-cut passages and tunnels to pray in these ancestral shrines.

Bet Giyorgis, the House of St George, is the most remarkable of all the churches. It is essentially a monolith, hewn from a single block of stone.

GREAT MOSQUE OF DJENNÉ

| Latitude 13°54'N Longitude 4°33'W |
| Location Central Mali, West Africa |
| Faith Islam |
| Built 1907 |
| Approximate area 5,625 square metres (60,550 sq ft) |
| Access Entry permitted to Muslims only |

It's barely dawn, but the old town of Djenné is abuzz with excited activity. Men are rushing along carrying enamel bowls and wicker baskets filled with wet mud, kicking up clouds of dust. Boys are tearing about with donkey carts, or jumping in pools of mud to keep it stirred, screaming with laughter. Women and girls, balancing buckets of water on their heads, dodge their way nimbly through the crowds. Drummers and pipers set up a cacophonous beat. They are all heading for the mosque, which is teeming with men clambering up slender palm-wood ladders and scaling the heights on the bundles of palm sticks that project from the walls. They pull handfuls of mud from the bowls proffered to them and smear it in thick layers onto the walls, onto the parapets, onto the crenellations and pinnacles, smoothing it down by hand.

This is the annual Fête de Crépissage (Festival of Rendering, or Plastering), and there's good-natured competition between the various quarters of the town for the honour of seeing which can do the work best. Time is also of the essence. It's March or April, the hot season, and the job has to be completed before the sun starts warming the walls. This is also an act of religious observance: the mosque is the heart and soul

The interior is a forest of pillars, tightly packed to support the heavy mud roof. Light enters from the spacious courtyard, the few windows, and holes pierced in the roof. Insulated by the thick walls from sounds from outside, there is a profound silence here, and a meditative calm enhanced by the timeless simplicity of the architecture, which is softened by the light and shadow of the twilight gloom.

The mosque is given a dynamic, bristling look by the rounded crenellations on the roofline and the ranks of projecting spars, which also serve a functional use as scaffolding.

of this ancient town, and participating in this energetic, sometimes dangerous work brings merit. And when it's all over, there's a party and a feast. Then the mosque will resume its role as a tranquil place of worship.

The Great Mosque of Djenné – the largest mud-brick building in the world – needs this kind of maintenance. Every year the heavy rains that fall between May and September erode the surface, while heat and humidity riddle it with cracks. The thick walls are made of sun-dried mud-bricks composed of clay silt from the nearby Bani River, mixed with rice husks, straw and cow dung for strength. Wet mud is plastered over the surfaces to create a smooth finish – lending the mosque an extraordinary, handmade, sculptural character, embellished by the rhythms of the small, oddly shaped windows and the

projecting spars of palm sticks that provide both structural support and scaffolding for maintenance work. The mosque looks ancient, but it was built in 1907. However, the story goes back much further than that. Djenné is probably the oldest city in sub-Saharan Africa, believed to have been

founded before 200 BC. Along with Timbuktu, 350 kilometres (220 miles) to the northeast, it prospered from the trans-Saharan trade in gold, ivory, salt and slaves, which – in the 13th century – brought in Islam. Djenné became a regional centre of Islamic learning, with madrassahs (Koranic schools) and a famous library – both of which it still has.

Legend recounts that the first king to convert to Islam pulled down his palace to build a mosque in its place. Another mosque superseded that one, but by the 19th century it was in a state of decayed ruin. It was under French colonial rule that the ambitious project to build a huge new mosque in local style took shape. The layout follows traditional Islamic patterns: within the walls is a large open courtyard, and then a covered prayer hall: cool and dark, lit by star-shaped ventilation holes in the mud-coated roof, supported by 90 pillars – there is space for 1,000 worshippers.

The people of Djenné are staunch traditionalists, restricting modernization to little more than a loudspeaker system for the call to prayer. Founded against the backdrop

The backs of the projecting towers, seen from the roof, show the sculptural work of many hand-palms over the decades, smoothing out the rounded shapes that are gentle on the eye, as well as wholly practical as weather-proofing.

of the desert, there is a disciplined, purist austerity at the heart of Islam. But that does not rule out fun, or the joy of community life – all of which comes to a head around the Great Mosque of Djenné at the annual Fête de Crépissage.

163

CHICHÉN ITZÁ

The Maya have had a knife-edge relationship with their gods. In all their mighty, city-states spread across Central America – Palenque, Tikal, Uxmal, Copán, Yaxchilán – the central buildings are massive stone temples or step-pyramids from which their priestly caste would try to appease the gods and ensure survival. Their complex calendar meshed two counting systems to produce a schedule of malign and propitious days, each to be respected with rituals performed by their élite: kings, nobles, warriors in their feathered finery, ornamented in gold. Bloodletting was an essential part of this appeasement, by self-mutilation and by human sacrifice. It is said that sacrificial victims went to their deaths gladly, proud to be chosen as messengers to the gods. Who is to say?

Chichén Itzá was the largest city in Maya lowlands, set on the dry limestone crust of the Yucatán Peninsula. Water was critical here, and its supply was assured by the presence of two large natural wells in sinkholes, called *cenotes*. Chichén (with emphasis of the last syllable) means 'mouth of the well'. Vital lifelines, these wells were sacred, and thought to be gateways to the underworld. Legend had it that virgin girls were ritually sacrificed in the larger of the two wells, the Cenote Sagrado, when the city faced drought. Or rather, they were thrown into the well at dawn, and any survivors were rescued at midday by ropes: they were then treated as sacred. These stories were dismissed as rumours until excavations in 1904–10 revealed skeletons, many of them female, along with various precious votive items, such as jewellery.

A ceremonial pathway led through the ordered city between the two *cenotes*, past the main pyramid, the Temple of Kukulkán, otherwise known as El Castillo (The Castle). It rises steeply to 24 metres (78 ft), with wide flights of 91 steps running up each of the four sides – a total of 364 steps, with

---

Latitude 20°40'N Longitude 88°34'W
Location Yucatán Peninsula, Mexico
Faith Maya
Built From C.AD 600
Approximate area 15.5 square kilometres (6 sq miles)
Access Ticketed entry daily

TRAVELLER'S **TIPS**

Best time to go: The winter months are best to avoid the summer heat, but December can be crowded. Stay a night and get into the park early, before the day-trippers from Cancún arrive.

Look out for: Below the pyramid temples, guides demonstrate how the echoes of hand-clapping sound like the birdcall of a quetzal, and, in another place, resemble a rattlesnake.

Dos and don'ts: Do not expect to climb up the Temple of Kukulkán (El Castillo) and the other larger monuments: this has been forbidden since 2006.

The design of the Temple of Kukulkán, the ceremonial centrepiece, incorporates some astronomical features that suggest it also functioned as an observatory, linking it to a calendar of rituals.

165

the top plinth making 365, the number of days in the year. The temple is set at an angle to true north. As a result, at the winter and autumn equinoxes, the sun hitting the chevroned corners of the pyramid casts a wavy shadow on the flat balustrade of the facing steps, building over several hours to a crescendo when the shadow links to a stone serpent's head at the foot of the steps. Kukulkán, the feathered serpent sky god, has returned to earth, ready to slither off into the *cenotes*. This event is celebrated at the equinoxes to this day by large crowds of revellers and sun-worshippers.

Another notable monument lies almost 1 kilometre (0.6 miles) to the southwest. It has a round building on the top, with a corbelled (stepped) roof creating a kind of dome effect (the Maya did not use the arch). Because of its shape, this structure is called El Caracol (The Snail), or the Observatory – and indeed it may have been used to track the movement of the stars and planets.

The Maya civilization collapsed in around AD 900 for reasons that remain a mystery. Chichén, however, lived on, and was taken over by the Itzá people (giving the city its second name), in alliance with the Toltecs – the new, militaristic rulers of northern Mexico. The Toltecs made roofed buildings using columns and crossbeams covered in palm thatch; these included the Temple of the Warriors and the complex called the Thousand Columns (actually 360), which probably served as a marketplace.

It seems that the Toltecs were ousted by a Maya chief in around 1220, but the city was in decline by the time the Spanish conquered the Yucatán in the 1530s. It was abandoned in the following decades, and the thatched, adobe dwellings crumbled. Invaded by scrubby woodland, Chichén Itzá became a forgotten ruin, until rediscovered in 1843. Although all we see now is bare stone, bereft of its paint and decoration and its throngs of richly adorned inhabitants, a powerful spirit of intent still animates Chichén Itzá.

No other surviving Maya building has the dome-like structure of the Observatory, which an inscribed slab dates to about AD 906. Its other name, El Caracol (The Snail), refers to the spiral staircase inside.

The figure known as Chac Mool appears widely in Toltec and other post-Classic Mayan sites across Mexico. He reclines on his back, knees up, head to one side, holding a platter on his chest. He was given this name by 19th-century archaeologists, and it was suggested the platter was a vessel to receive the hearts of the victims of human sacrifice. This is plausible – but in fact quite unproven.

Latitude 17°29'N **Longitude** 92°2'W	
Location Chiapas State, southern Mexico	
Faith Mayan	
Built From c.226 BC to 12th century AD	
Approximate area 25 square kilometres (9 sq miles)	
Access Ticket access, daily	

TRAVELLER'S TIPS

Best time to go: Winter (December to February) has the most comfortable temperatures. Summer is hot and humid.

Look out for: Palenque's site museum presents interesting artefacts from the excavations (sculpture, incense burners, death masks).

Dos and don'ts: Arrive at opening time (8 a.m.) to beat the tour buses: stay the night locally in order to be able to do this. Bring a hat, water and sunscreen.

PALENQUE

'Lost cities' are seldom truly lost. They are known to local people who have no idea of the excitement that the abandoned ruins will arouse in outsiders when they are brought to their knowledge. But the Mayan city of Palenque really does almost qualify for that label. Its own historical records run out in 1123. After that it was consumed by the voracious jungle of this hot and well-watered part of southern Mexico, until Spanish settlers stumbled upon it in the 1740s. Early reports and drawings of great temples and palaces excited the imaginations of readers in Europe and North America, already gripped by the poetic and exotic fantasies of Romanticism.

For more than a century Palenque continued to deliver intoxicating images of battered ruins cut out of the tropical forest, snarled in tree roots, and plastered with vivid images and strange hieroglyphs in stone and stucco relief, the meaning of which remained tantalizingly elusive. Serious archaeology began only in the 1930s, gradually bringing order to the chaos, and changing the ruins into the serene realm of lawn and shade that we see today.

As knowledge about Mayan culture was pieced together from the many other abandoned cities across southern Mexico, Honduras and Guatemala, and the hieroglyphs were deciphered, the story of Palenque unfurled. Here once had stood a great city, founded perhaps as early as the third century BC, reaching an apogee in AD 600–900, ruled by a dynasty of kings and queens bound by an intense covenant with their gods, which placed their temples at the heart of their culture. What we see today appears to be a rebuilding by a king called Kinich Janaab Pacal, also known as Pacal the Great, after destruction in a war with the rival city of Calakmul in AD 599–611. He had come to the throne aged 12 in 615 and ruled for 68 years.

Temples predominate. There is an impressive trio of stepped temples called the Temple of the Cross Group (after the Mayan World Tree symbol), which also has the Temple of the Foliated Cross and the Temple of the Sun, with an extravagant lattice roof comb. The most substantial complex is called the Palace; its unique, four-storey tower was perhaps used to make the astronomical observations that underpinned the complex Mayan calendar and cosmology. Most striking of all is the

The Palace appears to have had several functions, to judge from sculpted plaques and inscriptions found there. It may have served as both a royal residence and a temple: religion and secular life were closely interlinked.

Temple of the Inscriptions, with its line of five entrances decorated with panels that relate the story of the royal dynasty.

It took until 1952 to discover Palenque's greatest treasure. The panels of the Temple of the Inscriptions describe the central importance of Pacal the Great. When a stone floor slab was lifted, it revealed steps leading down to a crypt filled with rubble. At the bottom of this was a box containing six skeletons, male and female. A triangular slab of stone in the wall opened onto a funerary chamber and a sarcophagus with an intricately inscribed stone lid. This turned out to contain the skeleton of Pacal himself, complete with copious jade jewellery (the symbol of life and rejuvenation) and a death mask of jade, mother of pearl and obsidian, with haunting eyes of shell. Here were the mortal remains of the Maya's best-known king, the man portrayed widely across this city – with his prominent nose and flattened forehead (the attributes of ideal Mayan beauty) beneath his feather headdress – negotiating survival and prosperity with ancestor spirits and the gods. The skeletons at the entrance to the funerary chamber were, we can assume, sacrificial victims, despatched to accompany their king into the underworld.

Palenque delivers its secrets bit by bit – only the central area has so far been excavated, 200 structures out of perhaps 1,000, and one-tenth of the total area. What is yet to be discovered can only be imagined.

The Temple of the Inscriptions is the most impressive of the temples, and is a worthy, if secret, mausoleum for Pacal the Great.

The Temple of the Skull is so named because of this expressive stucco image, which appears at the foot of one of the pillars. In contrast to the customs of later Mesoamerican peoples, notably the Aztecs, the Mayans practised human sacrifice only rarely. However, ritual bloodletting, especially by royalty, was seen as an important way of propitiating the gods, and ensuring good fortune and continuity.

MACHU PICCHU

Latitude 13°09'S **Longitude** 72°32'W	
Location Central southern Peru	
Faith Inca	
Built c.1450	
Approximate area 5 hectares (12 acres). Park: 325 square kilometres (125 sq miles)	
Access Restricted entry by ticket, purchased in advance	

The Incas cut stone in irregular shapes, which keyed into each other for strength. They used harder stone and abrasion with sand to achieve a perfect, mortarless fit, no doubt tested repeatedly in the process. They also liked to shape stone with pillow-like edges.

If any spiritual place deserves to be called breathtaking, this is surely it. The ruined Inca town of Machu Picchu has an outstandingly dramatic setting, set on a saddleback ridge that plunges vertiginously 600 metres (2,000 ft) to the gorge of the foaming River Urubamba below. And it is 2,430 metres (7,972 ft) above sea level: as visitors move up and down the long flights of steps and look down on cloud banks and the backs of soaring condors, they may find it difficult to breathe the thin air.

Its extraordinary remoteness preserved this Inca town from discovery by the outside world for 400 years. Built by the Incas in around 1450, it thrived for 80 years, supporting a population of about 1,000. Then a small contingent of Spanish conquistadors led by Francisco Pizarro hoodwinked and defeated the Inca élite at Cajamarca in 1532 and their empire imploded. Although it lies only 70 kilometres (43 miles) northwest of the Inca ceremonial capital of Cuzco, the conquistadors never found Machu Picchu, but it was abandoned for unknown reasons in about 1570. It remained a local secret until a young American professor from Yale University called Hiram Bingham came across it in 1911. He and his team cleared and excavated the site the following year, and his reports and photographs printed in *National Geographic* excited the imagination of the world.

The Incas left no written records: much of our knowledge of their extraordinary civilization comes from Spanish reports in the immediate aftermath of conquest. For Machu Picchu there is a complete blank: all that can be deduced is what can be read from archaeological remains. The quality of the stonework in some of the buildings suggests that Machu Picchu had some religious significance. In their temples and palaces, as at Cuzco, the Incas used stone cut in polygonal shapes, carved with harder stone and bronze chisels and

A view from a vantage point above Machu Picchu shows how its terraces cling tightly to the contours of the saddle of the ridge.

knitted together without mortar. Some of the buildings at Machu Picchu show this distinctive style, notably the semicircular Temple of the Sun, so called because alignments with the solstices have been detected. Another intriguing feature is the Intihuantana, a piece of rock at the highest point of the 'Sacred District' of the town which has been carved into a distinctive pinnacle that aligns with the solstices; Intihuantana has been translated as 'Hitching Post of the Sun' because it is said to have controlled the passage of the sun across the heavens.

If that was indeed the belief, Machu Picchu would certainly have been a cult centre of extraordinary power. The term 'Inca' actually referred to their kings, who were treated as deities closely linked to the sun. Machu Picchu is thought to have

been founded by the first of these, the warlord Pachacuti Inca Yupanqui, who reigned from 1438 to 1471. One plausible theory is that Machu Picchu was an exclusive royal retreat, but that does not preclude it also being a site of religious significance. Astronomical alignments have been detected in the landscape itself: the distinctive peak of Huayna Picchu, which rises just to the northwest of the town, has a temple on the summit.

In the absence of any other evidence, all is speculation. Machu Picchu does, however, hold strong spiritual significance for indigenous Peruvians for another reason. This was an Inca site that the Spanish never found, so it has an untainted authenticity. Plunder came much later: Hiram Bingham and his team removed thousands of sophisticated artefacts but,

after a long campaign by Peru, in 2007 Yale University agreed to return them.

Efforts, too, have been made to preserve the authentic character of the site itself. Today visitor numbers are restricted to 2,500 per day. Some make the journey on foot along the Inca Trail from Cuzco; others go by train to nearby Aguas Calientes and then take a bus to the site. Machu Picchu is certainly not the virgin lost city that Hiram Bingham revealed to the world, but it still fills visitors with wonder and awe, and the mystery of unfathomable history.

There are about 140 stone buildings in Machu Picchu, suggesting that it had a permanent population of about 700 to 1,000.

LAKE TITICACA

To the Incas, this was where human life began – a vast, deep-blue lake splashed across a great treeless plain high in the Andes, next to the heavens. Here the supreme deity Viracocha rose from the earth and created the sun god Inti and installed him on the Isla del Sol, and the moon goddess Mama Quilla on the Isla de la Luna. His work done, he descended into the Pacific Ocean, leaving the Inca ('lord') to rule in his place.

Viracocha also built the temple at Tiahuanaco (or Tiwanaku), close to the lake shore, or created giants to do the work for him – for how else could this ancient construction of massive blocks of stone be explained? The Incas revered the temple as the source of their religion, but by the time they came to power in the 15th century – and rose to rule the largest Andean empire from their capital at Cuzco, 350 kilometres (220 miles) northwest of Lake Titicaca – Tiahuanaco had been a place of worship for perhaps 3,000 years. A large temple complex was built here from about AD 500, made of stone quarried some 90 kilometres (56 miles) away and, we presume,

Latitude 15°45'S **Longitude** 69°29'W	
Location Southeast Peru/western Bolivia	
Faith Andean religions	
Built Temples from c.AD 500	
Approximate area 8,372 square kilometres (3,232 sq miles)	
Access Free access to lake; ticketed entry to temples	

In calm repose, the lake stretches away from the shores of the Isla del Sol, one of the locations of the Inca creation myth. Here the sun and moon produced the Adam and Eve of Inca mythology.

The Uros people have been living on Lake Titicaca for more than 2,000 years, and consider themselves to be its guardians. They use totora reeds to create floating islands, and to build their houses, furniture and boats. The boats consist of long, tapering bundles of reeds, which are strapped together in a canoe shape, and are often paired to make a catamaran. The prows are decorated with simple and open-mouthed animal heads.

shipped in by raft – perhaps the same kind of reed rafts still used by the Uros people today. The hard stone was cut with harder stone into neat blocks with machine-flat surfaces and interlocking tenon joints, then carved with faces and stylized images of the gods.

Tiahuanaco now lies some 20 kilometres (12 miles) from the lake, separated from it by the mountain-building that continues to reshape the Andes. Its large, open and rather austere courtyards and gateways and monolithic statues stand with lips sealed, revealing little; there are no written records about the meaning of this place. Equally mysterious are the ruins of Puma Punku close by, with its huge blocks of stone carved into interlocking H-shapes.

A further piece of the puzzle was discovered in 2000: a huge underwater temple, perhaps 1,500 years old, at the end of an ancient causeway leading out into the lake from the Bolivian town of Copacabana. Religions of the Andes tended to focus on nature, with gods of the sun and sky, the forces of nature

and the mountains – the source of water so vital to their irrigated agriculture: beyond such clues, we can only speculate.

Now straddling the border between Bolivia and Peru, Lake Titicaca is still held sacred by the indigenous Aymara people who inhabit its shores and the surrounding Andes Altiplano (high plain). Each year, especially at the solstices, thousands make pilgrimages to the old Aymara and Inca temples on the Isla del Sol and the Isla de la Luna, and on many of the other 40 sacred islands. On Amantani island, the Fiesta de la Santa Tierra is celebrated every January with a pilgrimage and a race between two pre-Inca temples that crown peaks called Pacha Mama (Mother Earth) and Pacha Tata (Father Earth); the outcome will determine the success of the harvest.

The Uros people maintain a way of life on Lake Titicaca that pre-dates the Incas, on floating islands made of totora reeds. Their religion is a blend of Indian traditions and Catholicism. A similar blend is brought to the annual pilgrimages – in early February and early August – to Bolivia's most revered sacred

TRAVELLER'S TIPS

Best time to go: The dry season – May–September – is best. Heavy rains can be expected during the rest of the year.

Look out for: Boat trips to the floating Uros islands, departing from Puno (in Peru). You can arrange to stay on one of the islands, and learn more about their unique culture.

Dos and don'ts: Lake Titicaca is 3,812 metres (12,507 ft) above sea level, well above the altitude where mountain sickness might be expected. Make sure that you give yourself time to acclimatize.

image, the Virgin of the Candles at the Basilica of Copacabana. This statue of the Virgin Mary, carved from maguey wood in about 1576, is said to have the power to deliver miracles. Her feast day on 2 February is celebrated with a three-day festival of Aymara music, costume and dance, and a deep sense of sanctity – a complex mix of culture interwoven with time.

The floating islands of the Uros people are made of thick beds of reeds, which need to be constantly topped up to keep afloat. After about 20 years they become too waterlogged and have to be abandoned for a new island.

SUPERSTITION MOUNTAIN

Latitude 33°28'N **Longitude** 111°14'W
Location Central Arizona, southwest USA
Faith Native American Indian
Age c.1,000 years
Approximate area 650 square kilometres (250 sq miles)
Access Free access to the Superstition Wilderness Area

The Pima Indians warned the white settlers about it in the 1860s. This heavily eroded volcanic plug, rising 900 metres (3,000 ft) above the surrounding arid plains, was a place of unaccountable phenomena. It was the home of the Thunder God of their enemies, the Apache; it was riddled with portals to the underworld, and inhabited by mischievous 'little people' called Tuar-Tums, who protected its treasures. To the Pima, it was Ka-Katak-Tami, 'Crooked Top Mountain'; the white settlers renamed it 'Superstition Mountain'.

During the 18th century the mountains gained a reputation as a source of gold, setting the scene for conflict with the Apache. An expedition led by Mexican landowners was allegedly attacked and wiped out by Apache warriors in 1848. Other prospectors persisted, and some struck lucky, most famously an adventurer called Jacob Waltz. During the 1870s and 1880s, he would appear periodically in nearby Phoenix to spend his fortunes earned from high-grade gold ore. He is said to have killed about a dozen men to protect the secret location of his mother lode.

In 1891 he died of pneumonia in Phoenix, but not before telling his secret to the woman who nursed him, Julia Thomas. So began 'The Legend of the Dutchman's Lost Goldmine'. Julia Thomas and countless others scoured the area to find the gold, but none of the modest discoveries that resulted has been attested as the Dutchman's gold. Instead, a series of unexplained incidents – more than 50 disappearances and deaths – have been recorded at Superstition Mountain since the 1890s, reinforcing the legends of the 'Curse of the Apache Thunder God'.

Soaring cliff-faces and a barricade of teddy-bear cholla cactus conspire to give Superstition Mountain the kind of forbidding character that the Apache were content to promote in order to keep strangers out.

TRAVELLER'S TIPS

Best time to go: The Superstition Wilderness Area is considered to be a three-season hiking zone: autumn, winter and spring (October to May). Summer is dangerously hot.

Look out for: Petroglyphs (engraved images on rocks) featuring humans, deer and snakes; they can be seen on the 'Hieroglyphic Trail' and were made by the Hohokam ancestors of the Pima.

Dos and don'ts: Do go hiking on one of the many trails through the Superstition Wilderness Area. For family fun, see the Goldfield Ghost Town, a visitor attraction on the site of a mining town abandoned in 1926.

CRATER LAKE

Latitude 42°56'N **Longitude** 122°06'W	
Location Oregon, USA	
Faith Native American	
Age 7,000 years	
Approximate area 52 square kilometres (20 sq miles)	
Access The Crater Lake National Park is open all year (visitor centres close in winter)	

No one who visits Crater Lake can fail to see why the local Klamath people held it in such awe. This extinct volcano rises in a low-slung, tree-cloaked cone that rises to 2,438 metres (8,000 ft) above sea level at the highest point of the rim – a jagged ring of rock 10 kilometres (6 miles) across, with panoramic views over the Cascade Range and out to the Pacific Coast to the west. From here it plunges precipitously down into the crater where, 610 metres (2,000 ft) below, lies an ice-cold lake of startling sapphire blue. The only blemishes on the surface of the lake are the perfect mini-cone of Wizard Island, and the smaller island known as the Phantom Ship.

The air is bracing, the winds sometimes ferocious. Snow hugs the shadows even in summer, and blankets the landscape to a depth of up to 4 metres (13 ft) over a winter that lasts from October to May. In summer, electrical storms bounce and crackle around the hollow. August may be muffled in a thick fog. This is nature in its most unbound and commanding mode, witnessed in the dynamic shapes forged by cataclysmic volcanic eruption, and in a climate that can be beguilingly sweet but only if it so chooses.

The Klamath people, whose ancestors have lived in the region for 12,000 years, see spirit power in various natural phenomena. For them, Crater Lake is a place of power and danger. This is where individuals could (and still do) undertake spiritual 'vision quests', seeking enlightenment in the wilderness as a rite of passage. Shamans came here to test or renew their spiritual powers: swimming in the lake at night, underwater, where spirits roamed, was one of the most terrifying challenges. Their dreams at the lakeside were held as particularly potent, and would dictate their whole approach to medicine. The steep crater walls were treated as physical challenges, and those who triumphed unscathed in feats of endurance were held to have special spirit powers.

A volcano within a volcano, the neat cone of Wizard Island rises from the depths of the lake, seen here from behind a towering shard of volcanic andesite.

The distinctive purple pollen cones of the whitebark pine are among many remarkable features of the flora and fauna of Crater Lake, treasured for centuries by local Native Americans. Klamath shamans undertook 'vision quests' here, seeking spiritual interaction with nature, and adopting local animals that they dreamed of – black bears, elks, coyote, red-tailed hawks – as their alter egos to guide them in their medicine.

Legends explained how the crater was gouged out in a cosmic battle between Skell, lord of the world above ground – the world of birds and mammals – and Llao, evil lord of the underworld and his band of demons assisted by monstrous crayfish, which could leap out of the water and grab unsuspecting humans. Skell, the victor, destroyed Llao's home and threw his body into the lake, where his allies, the voracious crayfish, began feasting on his flesh, thinking this was Skell. They realized what they had done only when they came to the face, then fled in alarm. Wizard Island is all that remains of Llao's head.

There are many astonishing aspects of Crater Lake that the Klamath could only have guessed at. The lake is so cold and blue because it is so deep: at 594 metres (1,949 feet), it is the deepest freshwater lake in the USA. Yet it is entirely above sea level. No streams run into the lake: it is replenished each year by the rain and snow, which match almost exactly what is lost by evaporation. The lake and mountain were formed by the mega-eruption that, in about 4680 BC, destroyed and collapsed the posthumously named Mount Mazama, which had formerly risen to some 3,600 metres (12,000 ft). That was Llao's home.

Crater Lake received its first recorded visit by non-Native Americans in 1853: three gold prospectors. In 1902 it became the fifth National Park, and is now visited by half a million people a year. They drive around the rim, and walk down steep paths to the lake, where they can swim, go fishing or even scuba diving, or take boat trips to Wizard Island (from July to mid-September).

Crater Lake is on such an unearthly scale that it can absorb these numbers and still inspire awe and respect, and transmit a spiritual resonance that seems to touch the soul in a way that pre-dates religion.

TRAVELLER'S TIPS

Best time to go: July, August and early September are best, but temperatures average only 19°C (67°F), and there may be low cloud or fog. Snow can be expected from October to May.

Look out for: Open in the summer months only, the spectacular Rim Drive runs for 53 kilometres (33 miles) around the crater, with panoramic views in all directions.

Dos and don'ts: Do take warm clothes – or layers of clothing that you can adjust to meet the need. Even in summer, temperatures range from 4°C (40°F) to 27°C (80°F).

A dusting of snow lends the lake a subtle beauty, adding a crispness to the jagged rocks, while the low winter sun casts a warm glow above the serene waters surrounding Wizard Island.

CHACO CANYON

Latitude 36°3'N **Longitude** 107°57'W	
Location Northwest New Mexico, USA	
Faith Native American	
Built C.AD 900 to 1150	
Approximate area 137 square kilometres (53 sq miles)	
Access Park open all year; entrance fees apply, for 7-day permits	

Chaco Canyon ◇ · Albuquerque

USA

MEXICO

Some places seem to exude a sense of mystery. They seem to have soaked up centuries of human questing and longing, which then slowly leaches out over centuries more. Chaco Canyon is such a place. This intriguing and remote river valley in northwest New Mexico has the most extensive set of pre-Columbian ruins in the USA. Here you find the remains of dozens of villages (*pueblos*) and other archaeological sites.

The largest and most famous is Pueblo Bonito. Centrally located, on the northern side of the canyon, it has a typically D-shaped ground-plan encompassing a cluster of some 650 rooms – stacked to four storeys high around the perimeter – and probably housed between 800 and 1,000 people. It was built of sandstone blocks, mud mortar, and tree trunks carried in from forests 110 kilometres (70 miles) away. Analysis of the tree trunks has permitted precise dating: most of Pueblo Bonito was built between AD 919 and 1085.

There are 13 other large villages, known as 'great houses' – all of similar date but all subtly different – in the canyon itself and on the flat-topped surrounding hills called *mesas*: Chetro Ketl, Pueblo del Arroyo, Una Vida, Peñasco Blanco, Hungo Pavi and Pueblo Alto, to name but a few.

The pueblos were carefully sealed up and abandoned in around 1150 for reasons unknown – perhaps because a prolonged drought destroyed the irrigation-based agriculture, which had sustained the inhabitants with maize, squash and beans for some 250 years. Whatever the cause, the pueblos remained more or less unused, slowly crumbling away, and unknown until they were surveyed by a US Army detachment in 1849. Excavations have been carried out since the 1890s, but what took place here remains an enigma.

The most distinctive feature of the 'great houses' are the round chambers known as kivas, formerly roofed or underground. Entered from above, they recall the simple pit-dwellings that pre-dated Chaco Canyon's monuments, and are thought to be

The semicircular disc of Pueblo Bonito lies on the flat valley floor, hard up against the canyon walls.

Round kivas, formerly covered with flat roofs, were a prominent feature of the Great Houses of Chaco Canyon. There are no precise records about their function, but later Hopi and Pueblo peoples followed traditions in which kivas were used for spiritual ceremonies, prayer vigils, dance sessions and public gatherings, so it is assumed that Chaco Canyon's kivas served the same function.

ceremonial gathering places. Pueblo Bonito has some 40 kivas in total, including two 'great kivas'. Casa Rinconada, which is 800 metres (0.5 miles) from Pueblo Bonito, is the largest kiva in the canyon, and has no dwellings attached: measuring 19 metres (63 ft) in diameter, it could accommodate a gathering of perhaps 400 people.

As well as being a farming community, and a trading hub, importing such things as pottery, copper bells, and turquoise and seashells for jewellery, Chaco Canyon seems to have served as a spiritual centre. The buildings have been aligned to the points of the compass and movement of the sun, or to the extremes of the trajectory of the moon.

Rock-carvings and drawings in the canyon appear to underline this close interest in astronomical phenomena; this includes the famous 'Sun Dagger' carving high on the Fajada Butte, which registers the solstices and equinoxes.

A web of arrow-straight, meticulously constructed roads radiates out from the pueblos, and notably from Pueblo Alto, to distant 'outlier' pueblos and shrines that are situated in the desert beyond the canyon. Many of these could have served as roads, although they are strangely broad for a culture that had no wheeled vehicles; but others follow routes so steep that they could never have been practical as paths. They must – it has been surmised – surely have been some kind of spiritual paths, linking and binding together the key elements of the sacred landscape.

The Chacoan people who built these pueblos are often referred to as the Anasazi, meaning something like 'alien ancient ones' in Navajo. Pueblo cultures, such as the Hopi, and some clans of the Navajo, see the Anasazi as their forebears, who migrated out of Chaco Canyon in the 12th century and helped to found new groups across the area of the 'Four Corners', where New Mexico, Arizona, Utah and Colorado meet.

The customs and beliefs that these groups have preserved into modern times have been used to interpret many of the features of Chaco Canyon. Even if the picture remains unclear, the Hopi and Navajo see Chaco Canyon – protected since 1907 as a National Monument, and as the Chaco Culture National Historical Park since 1980 – as a sacred place of profound ancestral significance, which has to be treated with great respect and left as undisturbed as possible, for the spirits of their ancestors live on here.

The sun lights up the round walls of one of the kivas at Pueblo del Arroyo, near Pueblo Bonito. It was built between 1025 and 1125, close to the seasonal creek (*arroyo*) that runs through the middle of the canyon.

TRAVELLER'S **TIPS**

Best time to go: Chaco Canyon is 1,889 metres (6,200 ft) above sea level: very cold in winter, veering between very hot and cold in summer. Spring and autumn are more moderate, but can be wet.

Look out for: The Chaco Night Sky Program (April–October), operated by the Park's observatory, makes advantage of the Canyon's remoteness and lack of light pollution. Some 15,000 people participate every year.

Dos and don'ts: Spend at least a day at Chaco Canyon to see the main sights on the 14-kilometre (9-mile) loop road. Bring clothing for all weathers, even in summer.

INDEX

A

Abd al-Malik 133
Abd al-Rahman 48–51
Agion Oros, Greece 56–9
Agra, India 104–7
Aguas Calientes, Peru 175
Ahmet I 134–7
Al-Aqsa Mosque, Jerusalem 133
Al-Deir, Petra 125, 127
Al-Khazneh al-Faroun, Petra 127
Alexander II 68–71
Amritsar, India 100–3
Angkor Thom, Cambodia 92–3
Angkor Wat, Cambodia 90–3
Ashoka 95
Athens, Greece 60–1
Ayers Rock see Uluru
Ayvali, Cappadocia 143

B

Banon, Anilore 31
Beijing, China 72–3
Bernini 41
Besakih, Bali 112–15
Bet Giyorgis, Lalibela 156–9
Bingham, Hiram 172, 174–5
Blue Mosque, Istanbul 134–7
Bodh Gaya, India 94–5
Bodhi Tree, India 94–5
Borgund stave church,
    Norway 42–3
Borobudur, Indonesia 116–19
Bramante, Donato 42
Burckhardt, Johann Ludwig 127
Burgon, John William 127

C

Cairo, Egypt 149
Cajamarca, Peru 172
Camino Francés, Santiago de
    Compostela 44–7
Canaan, Egypt 152
Capernaum, Israel 129
Cappadocia, Turkey 142–5
Caracol, El, Chichén Itzá 166
Carnac, France 16–19
Castillo, El, Chichén Itzá 164–5
Cathar ruins, France 20–3
Cathedral of the Assumption of St Mary,
    Sergiyev Posad 67

Cathedral of the Holy Trinity, Sergiyev
    Posad 64–7
Cathedral of the Resurrection of Christ,
    St Petersburg 71
Cathédrale Notre-Dame, Chartres 25–9
Cavusin, Cappadocia 143
Cenote Sagrado, Chichén Itzá 164
Chaco Canyon, New Mexico, USA
    186–9
Charles V of Spain 51
Chartres Cathedral, France 24–7
Chichén Itzá, Mexico 164–7
Church of St Catherine, Egypt 152–5
Church of the Saviour on the Spilled Blood,
    St Petersburg, Russia 68–71
Colleville-sur-Mer, France 28–31
Copán, Honduras 164
Córdoba, Spain 48–51
Crater Lake, Oregon, USA 182–5
Cuzco, Peru 172, 175, 176

D

D-Day beaches, France 28–31
Dalai Lama 79–81
Darshani Deorhi, India 103
Derinkuyu, Cappadocia 145
Djenné, Great Mosque of 160–3
Dogubeyazit, Turkey 139, 140
Dome of the Rock, Jerusalem 130–3

E

Ein Musa, Petra 124
Elgin, Earl of 62
Elizabeth of Russia 67

F

Fátima, Portugal 52–5
Fête de Crépissage, Djenné 160–3

G

Galilee, Sea of, Israel 128–9
Ganges, India 96–9
Gebre Meskel Lalibela 156–9
Genghis Khan 146
Golden Hall, Wudang Mountains 77
Golden Pavilion, Japan 86–9
Golden Rock, Burma 110–11
Golden Temple of Amritsar,
    India 100–3
Gorëme, Turkey 142–5

Great Hall of Bulls, Lascaux 32–3
Great Mosque of Djenné,
    Mali 160–3
Gur-e Amir, Samarkand 146–7

H

Haçli, Cappadocia 143
Hajj, the 123
Hari Mandir Sahib (Golden Temple) 100–3
Hatshepsut 151
Hijra, the 121

I

Inca Trail 175
Innocent III 22
Iviron Monastery, Greece 58–9

J

Jabal an-Nour, near Mecca 123
Jerusalem, Israel 130–3
John Paul II, Pope 54
Jordon Rift Valley, Israel 128
Justinian I 154–5

K

Ka'aba, the 120–3
Karnak, Egypt 148–51
Kaymakli, Cappadocia 145
Kayseri, Cappadocia 143
Khor Virap, Armenia 139, 141
Kinich Janaab Pacal 169–71
Kinkaku-ji, Japan 86–9
Kinneret, Israel 128–9
Kiswah, the 122
Kora, the 79
Kyaikhtiyo, Burma 110–11
Kyoko-chi pond, Japan 86–8

L

Lake of Tiberias, Israel 128–9
Lake Titicaca, Peru/Bolivia 176–9
Lake Yamanaka, Japan 83
Lalibela, Ethiopia 156–9
Languedoc, France 21–2
Lao Tzu 75
Lascaux, France 32–3
Lhasa, Tibet, China 78–81
Lindisfarne, UK 12–15
Lourdes, France 34–7
Luxor, Egypt 148–51

M

Machu Picchu, Peru 172–5
Mahabodhi Temple, India 94–5
Maimonides 129
Marpo Ri, Lhasa 81
Masjid al-Haram, Mecca 120–3, 137
Mecca, Saudi Arabia 51, 120–3, 131, 133, 137
Medina, Saudi Arabia 121
Mehmet Agha 137
Mezquita de Córdoba, La, Spain 48–51
Michelangelo 41
Monastery, The, Petra 125, 127
Mount Agung, Bali 112–15
Mount Ararat, Turkey 138–41
Mount Athos, Greece 56–9
Mount Fuji, Japan 82–5
Mount Haku, Japan 82
Mount Meru, Cambodia 91
Mount of Mercy, near Mecca 123
Mount Sinai, Egypt 152–5
Mount Tate, Japan 82
Mumtaz Mahal 104–7
Muzdalifah, near Mecca 123

N

Nile, Egypt 151
Noble Sanctuary, Jerusalem 133
Normandy American Cemetery, France 30

O

Omaha Beach, France 28–31
Özkonak, Cappadocia 145

P

Pacal the Great 169–71
Pachacuti Inca Yupanqui 174
Palenque, Mexico 168–71
Parthenon, Greece 60–3
Petra, Jordan 124–7
Pizarro, Francisco 172
Plain of Arafat, near Mecca 123
Potala Palace, Lhasa, Tibet, China 78–81
Precinct of Amun, Karnak 151
Precinct of Montu, Karnak 151
Precint of Mut, Karnak 151
Purple Heaven Palace, Wudang Mountains 77

R

Raffles, Sir Thomas Stamford 119
Rambam 129
Ramses III, temple of 151
Ranjit Singh 101
River Ganges, India 96–9
River Nile, Egypt 151
Roha, Ethiopia 156–9
Rome, Italy 38–41
Rose Valley, Cappadocia 143

S

Saladin 129, 159
Samarkand, Uzbekistan 146–7
Santiago de Compostela, Spain 44–7
Santos, Lúcia 52–5
Sea of Galilee, Israel 128–9
Sergiyev Posad, Russia 64–7
Seti II, temple of 151
Shah Jehan 104–7
Shakhi-Zinda, Samarkand 146
Shiraito Falls, Japan 83
Simonos Petras 56–7
Songtsen Gampo 81
Soubirous, Bernadette 34–5
St Basil the Great 143
St Catherine's Monastery, Egypt 154–5
St Gregory the Illuminator 139, 141
St James 46–7
St Peter's Basilica, Vatican City 39–41
St Peter's Square, Vatican City 38–41
St Petersburg, Russia 68–71
St Sergius 65–7
Stave church, Borgund 42–3
Stonehenge, UK 8–11
Suleiman the Magnificent 133, 137
Sultan Ahmet Mosque, Istanbul 134–7
Superstition Mountain, Arizona, USA 180–1
Suryavarman II 91

T

Taj Mahal, Agra, India 104–7
Tamerlane 146
Ta Prohm temple, Angkor Wat 93
Temple of Heaven, Beijing, China 72–5
Temple of Kukulkán, Chichén Itzá 164–5
Temple of Olympian Zeus, Athens 63
Temple of the Cross Group, Palenque 169
Temple of the Foliated Cross, Palenque 169
Temple of the Inscriptions, Palenque 169–70

Temple of the Skull, Palenque 171
Temple of the Sun, Machu Picchu 174
Temple of the Sun, Palenque 169
Temple of Warriors, Chichén Itzá 166–7
Thebes, Egypt 148–51
Thomas, Julia 180
Thousand Columns, Chichén Itzá 166
Tiahuanaco, Bolivia 176
Tiberias, Israel 128–9
Tikal, Guatemala 164
Tonlé Sap, Cambodia 90
Treasury, The, Petra 127
Trinity Monastery, Sergiyev Posad 64–7
Tuthmosis III 151

U

Uluru, Australia 108–9
Uxmal, Mexico 164

V

Valley of Moses, Petra 124
Varanasi, India 96–9
Vatican City, Italy 38–41

W

Wadi Musa, Petra 124
Waltz, Jacob 180
Well of Moses, Petra 124
Well of Zamzam, Mecca 123
Western (Wailing) Wall, Jerusalem 131, 133
Wizard Island, USA 182–5
Woodhenge, UK 11
Wudang Mountains, China 74–7

X

Xuxu Palace, Wudang Mountains 76

Y

Yaxchilán, Mexico 164
Yoshimitsu, Ashikaga 86–8
Yucatán Peninsula, Mexico 164

Z

Zixiao Taoist temple, Wudang Mountains 77

ACKNOWLEDGEMENTS

Quercus Editions Ltd
55 Baker Street
7th Floor, South Block
London
W1U 8EW

First published in 2014

Copyright © Quercus Editions Ltd 2014
Text by Antony Mason

The picture credits constitute an extension to this
copyright notice.

Every effort has been made to contact copyright
holders. However, the publishers will be glad to
rectify in future editions any inadvertent omissions
brought to their attention.

Quercus Editions Ltd hereby exclude all liability
to the extent permitted by law for any errors or
omissions in this book and for any loss, damage or
expense (whether direct or indirect) suffered by a
third party relying on any information contained
in this book.

A catalogue record of this book is available from
the British Library

UK and associated territories:
ISBN 978 1 78206 854 9

Printed in Hong Kong

10 9 8 7 6 5 4 3 2 1

Printed and bound in Hong Kong
by Great Wall Printing Co. Ltd

Maps by Map Graphics Limited

Picture credits

GI = Getty Images

2–3 Thomas Barwick/GI 8–9 David Nunuk/GI
10–11 The Image Bank/GI 12–13 Steve Allen/GI
14–15 Arcaid/GI 15 Lee Frost/GI 16 Hiroshi
Higuchi/GI 16–17 Slow Images/GI
18–19 Oric1–Flickr/GI 20–1 Samuel Magal/GI
22 Fco. Javier Sobrino/GI 22–3 David Clapp/GI
24–5 Julian Elliott Ethereal Light/GI
26 Godong/GI 26–7 Travel Pix Collection/Awl
Images 28–9 Julio Lopez Saguar/GI 30 Louise
Heusinkveld/GI 30–1 Louise Heusinkveld/GI
32–3 DEA/G. Dagli Orti/GI 34–5 Sonnet
Sylvain/GI 36 Godong/GI 36–7 Paul Biris/GI
38–9 Buena Vista Images/GI 40–1 Massimo
Sestini/AFP/GI 41 Gonzalo Azumendi/GI
42–3 Frank van Groen/GI 44–5 John Harper/GI
46–7 by Lansbricae (Luis Leclere)/GI 47 Wayne
Walton/GI 48–9 Alex Linghorn/GI 50 DEA /
C. Sappa/GI 50–1 Mattes René/hemis.fr/GI
52–3 Mariusz Kluzniak/GI 54 Horst Neumann/
GI 54–5 Dmitry Shakin/GI 56–7 ©Dimitris
Sotiropoulos Photography/GI 58–9 ©Dimitris
Sotiropoulos Photography/GI 60–1 Scott E.
Barbour/GI 62–3 Dennis Macdonald 63 altrendo
travel/GI 64–5 Gavin Hellier/GI 66, 66–7 Ivan
Vdovin/GI 68–9 Pola Damonte/GI 70–1 Geoff
Tompkinson/GI 71 Keren Su/GI 72–3 Ilya
Terentyev/GI 74–5 Karl Johaentges/GI 76–7, 77
Keren Su/GI 78 Michael S. Yamashita/GI
79 Feng Wei Photography/GI 80–1 D E Cox/GI
82–3 Katsumi Takahashi/GI 83 Ippei Naoi/GI
84–5 Hiroshi Higuchi/GI 86–7 David Clapp/GI
86 John S. Lander/GI 88–9 David Clapp/GI
90–1 De Agostini/GI 92–3 Ignacio Palacios/GI
93 Daniel Cheong/GI 94–5 Jochen Schlenker/GI
95 Jonathan Clark/GI 96–7 Body Philippe/ hemis.
fr/GI 98 narvikk/GI 98–9 Dominik Eckelt/GI
100–1 Westend61/GI 102–3 AFP/GI/
103 Alan Lagadu/GI 104–5 David Pedre/GI
106–7 Christine Pemberton/GI 108–9 Brandon
Rosenblum 109 Richard I'Anson 110–11 Angelo
Cavalli/GI 111 Andrea Pistolesi/GI 112–13 Dirk
Wüstenhagen Imagery/GI 114–5 Michael
Freeman/GI 115 Richard I'Anson/GI 116–7 Paul
Biris/GI 117 Kimberley Coole/GI 118–19 Albert
Tan photo/GI 120–1 © Kazuyoshi Nomachi/
Corbis 122 © Susan Baaghil /Reuters/Corbis
122–3 Asif Waseem/Shutterstock 124–5 Martin
Child/GI 126–7 Galdric Pons/GI 127 Edden Ram
Photography/GI 128–9 Jon Arnold/GI
130–1 Reyaz Limalia/GI 132–3 Walter Bibikow/
GI 133 Hanan Isachar/GI 134 Bernardo Ricci
Armani/GI 134–5 Peter Adams/GI 136–7 Gardel
Bertrand / hemis.fr/GI 138–9 Martin Gray/GI
140 Jean-Bernard Carillet/GI 140–1 Tim Barker/
GI 142–3 Paul Nevin/GI 143 John and Tina Reid/
GI 144–5 Lemaire Stephane/hemis.fr/GI
146–7 Torsten Stahlberg/GI 148–9 Brian
Lawrence/GI 150–1 Cynthia Edorh/GI
151 Max Alexander/GI 152–3 Jon Arnold/GI
154 Danita Delimont/GI 154–5 James Baigrie/GI
156–7 Georges Courreges/GI 158–9 Klaas
Lingbeek van Kranen/GI 159 Andrew Holt/GI
160 Yann Doelan/GI 160–1 Image Source/GI
162–3 Yann Doelan/GI 164–5 Richard Nowitz/GI
166–7 Glow Images/GI 167 Chris Cheadle/GI
168–9 DEA Picture Library/GI 170–1 Arturo
Peña Romano Medina/GI 171 Danita Delimont/
GI 172 PeskyMonkey/GI 172–3 Sean Caffrey/GI
174–5 traveler1116/GI 176–7 Andras Jancsik/GI
178 Sean Caffrey/GI 178–9 traveler1116/GI
180–1, 182–3 Tim Fitzharris/GI 183 Bob Stefko/
GI 184–5 Sara Winter/GI 186–7 David Hiser/GI
187 Ralph Lee Hopkins/GI 188–9 David H.
Collier/GI

Title page: Stepping stones curve through a calm
lake towards mountains in Utah.